The

BOOK

of

PRAYERS

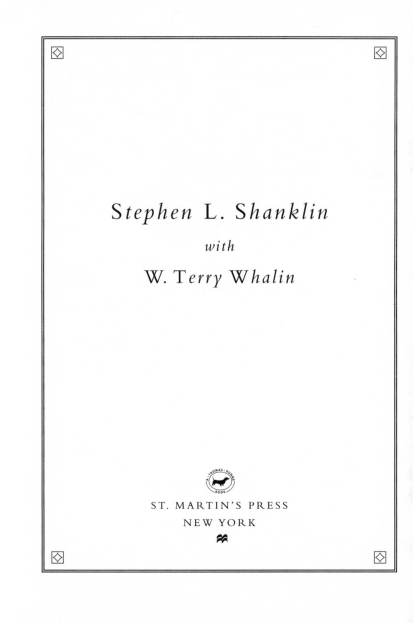

Stephen L. Shanklin

with

W. Terry Whalin

A THOMAS DUNNE BOOK

ST. MARTIN'S PRESS

NEW YORK

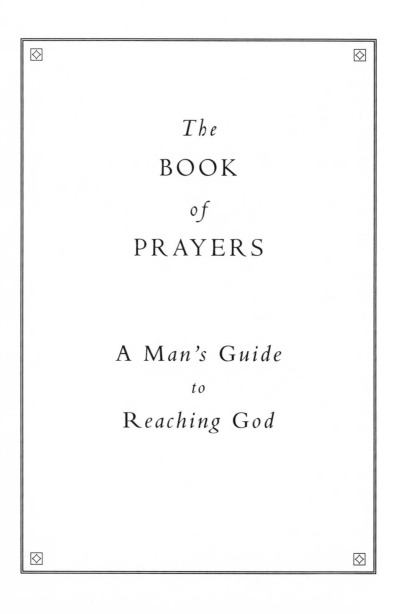

The

BOOK

of

PRAYERS

A *Man's Guide*

to

Reaching God

A THOMAS DUNNE BOOK.
An imprint of St. Martin's Press.

Design by MAUREEN TROY

Library of Congress Cataloging-in-Publication Data

Shanklin, Stephen L.
    The book of prayers : a man's guide to reaching God / by Stephen L. Shanklin with W. Terry Whalin.—1st ed.
        p.   cm.
    "A Thomas Dunne book."
    ISBN 0-312-18059-4
    1. Prayers.   I. Whalin, Terry.   II. Title.
    BV245.S46   1998
    242'.842—dc21   97-38127
                                                                      CIP

First Edition: February 1998

10   9   8   7   6   5   4   3   2   1

*This book is dedicated to Almighty God, to
whom all prayers are directed and from whom all answers come.
To my mother, Hazel Ruth Shanklin, who taught me the value of
persistent prayer. To Dad and Mom Gladney, who have given us a
constant stream of love and support.
To my wife, Denise, who has never failed to pray for me,
and to my twin boys, Gabriel and Christian,
who keep me on my knees.*

A c k n o w l e d g m e n t s

My special thanks to Dale Schlafer of Promise Keepers,
who gave me an opportunity to serve along with him
and call men of the nation to a life of prayer.
And my appreciation to Eddie Smith and his wife Alice,
my partners in prayer.
To my faithful brother in the Lord,
Daniel Paxton, who has been a source of strength.
To Scott Waxman, my literary agent, thank you for diligently
working to find a publisher for The Book of Prayers. *And to*
Neal Bascomb, our editor, thank you for carrying the enthusiasm
for this book at St. Martin's and your excellent editorial work.
Thank you, W. Terry Whalin, for the many hours
you prayerfully spent working on this project.
God bless!

Contents

Key to Abbreviations throughout
The Book of Prayers

NASB
New American Standard Bible

NCV
New Century Version

NIV
New International Version

NKJV
New King James Version

NLT
New Living Translation

TLB
The Living Bible

The
BOOK
of
PRAYERS

Foreword by
Coach Bill McCartney

◇

For a man, the best way to truly know God intimately is through prayer. As a football player, then a football coach for a major university, I learned that discipline causes a man to succeed in life, in particular the discipline of prayer. Every man needs the discipline of prayer.

The Bible tells us that very early in the morning, Jesus arose, left the house and went off to a solitary place where he prayed. (Mark 1:35) Prayer is not just communication; it is communion with God. It is in the place of prayer that a man gains the strength to live out his promises. I have always believed that communication with Almighty God is a sign of strength in a man.

Promise Keepers began and has experienced its phenomenal growth primarily because of prayer. In 1995, Promise Keepers saw the need to bring on a man that would help us enlarge our prayer efforts. This man was Stephen Shanklin. I can remember when Stephen and I first met how excited I was to hear his heart concerning mobilizing prayer for this nation and calling men to a higher prayer commitment in their personal lives.

Stephen and I have talked and prayed together on many occasions that Almighty God would touch the heart of men everywhere to become passionate about their personal prayer time with God. I believe that a man's highest priority should be coming before God in the morning.

When I discovered how sweet it was to reach God in prayer, I knew this was the place God had for me. This book, *The Book of Prayers: A Man's Guide to Reaching God*, is filled with fascinating stories of the difference that prayer can make in a man's life with more than one hundred spiritual prayers to guide a man toward reaching God.

Today, because of prayer, I can say that I am exactly where I am supposed to be, doing exactly what God created me to do. No victory on the gridiron, no coaching award, anything on earth, approaches the sheer delight of calling his name and hearing his soft reply. God alone knows what blessings are in store for those willing to commit to a life of prayer.

I challenge you—find out! This book is a very useful guide to assist you in developing a more intimate relationship with Almighty God. I believe Stephen has captured the very heart of God by giving men a prayer reference tool that will be a part of his life and his prayer relationship with God.

COACH BILL MCCARTNEY
FOUNDER OF PROMISE KEEPERS
SEPTEMBER 1997

CHAPTER 1

The Crucial Connection

◇

When have men turned to God in prayer? One significant event came during a bitter debate at the Philadelphia Constitutional Convention in 1787. Half of the New York delegates left the meeting in disgust and others threatened to leave. Suddenly everything changed from an unlikely speaker—an eighty-one-year-old statesman named Benjamin Franklin.

In a quiet voice, he spoke. "In the beginning of the contest with Britain, when we were sensible of danger, we had daily prayers in this room for Divine protection. Our prayers, sirs, were heard, and they were graciously answered. . . . And have we now forgotten this powerful Friend? Or do we imagine we no longer need His assistance?"

He paused to give his words some impact, then continued. "I have lived, sir, for a long time, and the longer I live, the more convincing proofs I see of this truth: that God governs in the affairs of man." Finally Franklin pleaded with the assembly to begin each day in prayer. The Founding Fathers turned to God in prayer and their actions carried through the early days of America.

Almost a hundred years later, pastor and chaplain in the Confederate army, E. M. Bounds said, "A man's strength develops in the place of prayer with God. Men who are strong in everything else ought to be strong in prayer. Men who are brave, persistent, illustrious in other pursuits ought to be full of courage, unfainting, strong-hearted in prayer."

Prayer has been instrumental in my own life. At the tender age of six, I stumbled out of bed one night and saw Mom praying on her knees. I wandered over and fell on my knees and joined her praying for a short time. As a child, it was easy through prayer to trust God for our needs. From early morning until late at night, my mother prayed for our family and from her example taught me the importance of prayer.

From her prayers, I grew aware of my own need for a personal relationship with God through Jesus Christ. My mother regularly told me, "Son, you can believe God for anything; all things are possible through Christ and prayer." As a young man growing up in a small Texas city, I was active in 4-H and longed to raise livestock. Unfortunately we had no land for animals nor could my parents afford them. At age ten, I asked God to give me some livestock. Two years later, God answered that prayer. Our family moved to ten acres of land and my parents purchased a Chester white Show Barrow pig, Mr. Twiggs, that I raised in cooperation with the Future Farmers of America program. Later that year, I entered Mr. Twiggs in the county fair and won the reserve grand champion with a prize of $3,000. In the mid-1960s, it was unheard of for an African American boy to win this type of contest. I attributed my victory to a lesson in prayer and God's provision.

BEYOND DESPERATION

All too often prayer is an emergency measure when a situation grows beyond hope. We call out, "Help me, God." I've known the desperation of prayer from the early years of my life. As a twelve-

2

year-old, I took my mom's dog, Sheba, near the street. Mom had warned me not to let our German shepherd outside our property. In horror, I watched a large log truck strike our dog. He couldn't move his back legs without great effort. Unless a miracle took place, I would be in immense trouble with my parents and my mother's dog wouldn't survive. I knelt on the street, and placed my hands on Sheba's head with tears running down my cheeks and started to pray: "O, God, Sheba needs your touch of healing. I ask it in the name of Jesus."

Then I stood and confidently called for Sheba. The dog began to stir. I continued calling and encouraging Sheba to move. The large dog staggered to his feet and began to wobble toward me. In a matter of minutes, Sheba completely recovered and I knew God heard my childhood prayers of desperation.

Whether with animals or human relationships, there are times for desperate prayer. Also from my experience, a man's strength comes from prayer throughout life—in times of sorrow and rejoicing. In prayer, a man can achieve success in the arena of life. 1 Timothy 2:8 (NLT) reveals God's desire for men to pray, saying, "I want men to pray with holy hands lifted up to God, free from anger and controversy." A man who is committed to prayer can succeed when others fail and win the triumphs of life. Praying men are God's chosen leaders. It does not matter to God the culture of a man, his education, or his race because it is through prayer that God single-handedly develops his warrior.

Across the nation, I've seen a great increase in the number of men who are surrendering to the life and call of prayer. These men are becoming strong leaders in their homes and in the nation. For a moment, let's consider some of the great leaders from the Bible. Moses would not have been a great leader if he had not been committed to a life of prayer. The prophet Elijah, who entered heaven on a chariot of fire, would not have been listed in the Hall of Great Victories (Hebrews 11:1–40) without his communication with God.

Many of the great leaders of the church were committed to spending time in prayer—men like Martin Luther, John Wesley, Charles Finney, or Billy Graham. These men became leaders as they came to God in prayer. When confronted with great problems or challenges, they turned to their Heavenly Father. In Ecclesiastes 3:11 (NKJV), the Lord says that "he has put eternity in their hearts" and moves mankind in an upward pull through the communication of prayer. The early church father Augustine said, "There is a God-shaped vacuum in every man that only Christ can fill."

From my personal experiences with prayer, I was propelled to study the great men of prayer and model their relationship with God. As I read about men like Praying Hyde, John Calvin, Jonathan Edwards, Charles Spurgeon, and Dr. J. Edwin Orr, my passion to know God through prayer increased. Early in my youth, I had learned that the Lord hears our prayers and answers them. The Bible says that faith comes from hearing, and hearing from the Word of God. I had heard these verses quoted thousands of times in my home. From the example of my mother, I learned to stretch my faith toward the heavens and reach God through prayer. Later, as I grew to manhood, prayer became an integral part of my daily life. Unfortunately, too many men delay turning to God in prayer until there is a difficulty in life. They reserve prayer for a last-minute resort instead of a constant, steady stream of conversation with the Heavenly Father.

The Book of Prayers: A Man's Guide to Reaching God has been developed to help you communicate with God in prayer on a consistent basis. As you use these various chapters, you may turn to God in your weakness, fears, pressures, and anxiety. Through prayer, these weaknesses are exchanged for God's strength. As a man prays, it releases his true spiritual desire to be strong. Because God commands us to pray and also gives us the privilege of prayer, this book assists you to turn to God. James 5:14–18 (NASB) tells us that "the prayer of a righteous man can accomplish much." As we pray through the various aspects of life, we become God's agents and ambassadors on earth.

Prayer is not a fruitless exercise. Instead prayer becomes a man's connection to the realm of the eternal and his means to find spiritual fulfillment. The apostle Paul said that men should "fight the good fight of faith." As men, we must make a concerted effort to pray and become faithful in our prayers. This guide prepares you to become a man of prayer.

CHAPTER 2

How to Pray

⊠

One day, three ministers were discussing various aspects of prayer and how to be effective. As they talked, a telephone repairman slipped into the room and was working on the phone in the background.

"I feel like the key to prayer is in the hands," one minister explained, and then demonstrated how he held his hands together and pointed them upward in symbolic worship.

"That's fine for you, but I've found my most effective prayer is on my knees," the second minister said. "It's through this humble act of kneeling that I can concentrate on communication with Father God."

Not to be outdone by the other two men and their knowledge of prayer, the third minister chimed in to the conversation, "I think you've both got it wrong. The only position that I've found worth its salt for prayer is to be stretched out on the floor flat on your face before God's throne."

Finally the telephone repairman couldn't keep silent. He said, "I've found the most effective prayer I ever made was while I was dangling upside down by my heels from a power pole suspended forty feet above the ground!"

There are many different styles and location for prayer. Whichever you select, it's the bottom line that matters—we are communicating with God. Dr. J. Edwin Orr, the great historian on the subject of prayer, during one of his lectures said, "Whenever God is going to do something among his people, he always starts them praying."

As I have traveled the nation, talking about prayer, praying with different men and organizing a large prayer movement for Promise Keepers, I've seen a new hunger stirring across the nation among men for prayer. These men desire to understand how to pray and how to sustain the daily discipline of an effective prayer life. Through their devotion to God, men are seeking a deeper relationship with God. Prayer is a means to find that relationship.

Christian leaders like John Maxwell, while serving as the senior pastor of Skyline Wesleyan Church in San Diego, began a vibrant prayer ministry. The meetings began small but soon grew to over one hundred men who are devoted to prayer. Across the land, a fresh wind is blowing to call men to pray.

Through prayer a man is able to

- communicate with the Creator of the Universe;
- consistently develop a regular communication pattern with God;
- move his life and emotions closer to God's desires instead of his own.

How does a man become a prayer warrior? Like a warrior prepares for battle, the first step is for a man to focus on the importance of prayer. Whether you pray early in the morning or late at night, God's presence can fill your life.

As a small boy, I heard my mother say, "Steve, little prayer, little power. Much prayer, much power. No prayer, no power."

From those words spoken three decades ago, I've seen the reality of prayer in my own life. I confess that I don't have all the answers or insight about this topic of prayer. My own life has whirled through numerous learning curves and growth, yet the fundamentals of prayer have been an anchor in trials and tests. My relationship with God has deepened and reached a new level of intimacy.

Through my time in prayer, I've learned that prayer is more than a constant asking from God. It involves building a relationship where you receive but also give. This chapter explores the various disciplines of prayer. As Jesus Christ walked the earth, on a hot, dusty day, his disciples approached him and asked, "Lord, teach us to pray." The disciples learned about prayer from the Master. In the same manner, we will turn to the Bible for instruction on the various aspects of prayer—length of prayers, when to pray, and which stance to use in prayer. The following pages include some fundamentals on prayer which will help you make more effective use of the remainder of the book.

How Long Should I Pray?

There are many schools of thought about the length of prayer. Some individuals extol the value of spending extended time in prayer while many others are left feeling guilty because they often struggle to pray for a few minutes.

If you selected a day and asked men from both sides (lengthy prayers or brief prayers), "How long have you prayed?" the common response would be one of dissatisfaction with the length of their prayers. Most men feel like they are not spending an adequate amount of time in communication with God.

As men, our daily challenge is to fulfill this need for more time in prayer. That time should not be spent asking from God but instead seeking for God to stretch our vision and to bless our communication. So often, our spirit is willing but our flesh or physical energy is weak. (Matthew 26:41) As David wrote in Psalm 42:1–3, (NLT), "As the deer pants for streams of water, so I long for you, O God. I thirst for God, the living God. When can I come and stand before him? Day and night, I have only tears for food, while my enemies continually taunt me, saying, 'Where is this God of yours?' "

When Jesus Christ was on the earth, he challenged his disciples on the subject of prayer. He asked them to pray, then he questioned them again when they fell asleep and didn't pray. Jesus said, "Couldn't you stay awake and watch with me even one hour?" (Matthew 26:40, NLT)

Now, Jesus himself was truly a man of prayer. Prayer characterized his life. As men, we should follow the example of Christ. His time of communication with his Heavenly Father was not optional, for it was through prayer that Jesus found his life in the Spirit. The more we give to God, the more we obtain from God.

Jesus challenged his disciples to pray with him for *one hour*. At first observation, this appears to be a great commitment. However the request is obtainable—otherwise Jesus would never have asked his disciples to pray for this length of time. The proof of our pursuit of a relationship with God is our commitment—which is spelled T-I-M-E. As David Brainerd, the colonial evangelist, wrote, "Oh, one hour with God, infinitely exceeds all the pleasures and delights of this lower world."

I will be the first to admit that the discipline to pray for one hour doesn't occur instantly or overnight. However, if you stay with this discipline and commitment to a spiritual relationship with the Creator, little by little your prayer time will increase. Gradually, you will eagerly anticipate this personal fulfillment. The strength and presence of God will lift you beyond complacency and procrastination to a commitment in prayer.

I have always used this exhortation from Jesus to his disciples about praying for an hour as *a goal* for my prayer life. At seminars on prayer, I have taught students how to develop quality time with

9

God. My advice is to start from where you are right now. If you pray for five minutes, then become faithful and add until you achieve your desired goal for the length of time in prayer. Jesus said, in Luke 14:28 (NLT), "But don't begin until you count the cost. For who would begin construction of a building without first getting estimates and then checking to see if there is enough money to pay the bills?" As men of prayer, if we are going to finish strong, we must make some definite changes to our life—spiritually, mentally, and emotionally. As Richard J. Foster says, "To pray is to change. Prayer is the central avenue God uses to transform us. If we are unwilling to change, we will abandon prayer as a noticeable characteristic of our lives. The closer we come to the heartbeat of God, the more we see our need and more we desire to be conformed to Christ. To pray is to change."

Suggestions for Prayer

1. Begin by setting a specific time for prayer.
2. Secure a comfortable location.
3. Pray until you have the assurance or until you feel a release from the Lord.
4. Pray until you see the answer.
5. Pray until you have a level of internal peace.
6. Pray until you receive the Lord's wisdom and direction.
7. Pray faithfully. Be persistent and focused—especially when the answer is delayed.

Jesus Christ encouraged men to pray for different lengths of time. Notice these italicized words from Jesus—ask, look, and knock, "And so I tell you, keep on *asking*, and you will be given what you ask for. Keep on *looking*, and you will find. Keep on *knocking*, and the door will be opened. For everyone who asks, receives. Everyone who seeks, finds. And the door is opened to everyone who knocks." (Luke 11:9–10, NLT)

When to Pray?

1. Develop and establish a *daily* and habitual prayer time.
2. Pray when you feel that the Lord is leading you to pray.
3. Pray when you are filled with anxiety and worry.
4. Pray when you are battling temptation.
5. Pray when you are faced with various decisions.
6. Pray when the Lord brings someone into your heart or mind.
7. Pray when you sense danger.
8. Pray in accordance with your natural body rhythm: i.e., if you are a morning person, then pray in the morning; or, if you are a night person, then pray at night.
9. Pray without ceasing!
10. Pray when you need deliverance from a particularly troublesome situation.

What the Bible Says About When to Pray

1. Pray all the time or without ceasing. In several places the Bible refers to the concept of praying all the time, and, at first glance, you may think this means every man enters a monastery. Instead this concept refers to an attitude about prayer. The constant dialogue with Heavenly Father doesn't have to occur at a particular time of day or night. Certainly sometimes formal prayers are given in a house of God or another setting. As men, we need to develop an attitude of prayer so we pray without ceasing.

The example of Paul:

"*Pray at all times and on every occasion* in the power of the Holy Spirit. Stay alert and be persistent in your prayers for all Christians everywhere." (Ephesians 6:18, NLT)

The example of Jesus:

"One day . . . Jesus went to a mountain to pray, and *he prayed to God all night*." (Luke 6:12, NLT)

The example of the Roman soldier Cornelius:

"In Caesarea there lived a Roman army officer named Cornelius, who was a captain of the Italian Regiment. He was *a devout man* who feared the God of Israel, as did his entire household. He gave generously to charity and was a man *who regularly prayed to God.*" (Acts 10:1–2, NLT)

Early-morning Prayer

The beginning of our day is an excellent starting point for prayer. In numerous places, the Bible refers to early-morning prayer and here are a couple of illustrations:

"But, Lord, I have called out to you for help; *every morning I pray to you.*" (Psalm 88:13, NCV)

"The next *morning* Jesus awoke long before daybreak and went out alone into the wilderness to pray." (Mark 1:35, NLT)

Noon Prayer

In the middle portion of our day or at noon is another excellent time to turn our thoughts to God in prayer. These are not prayers in a ritualistic sense of duty but prayers in devotion and love of God. "Morning, *noon,* and night I plead aloud in my distress, and the Lord hears my voice." (Psalm 55:17, NLT)

Night Prayer

What are you thinking about as you drift into sleep or in the final moments of your day? The researchers have proven that if we are struggling with a particular problem or situation, our subconscious takes over and continues wrestling with it throughout the night. The Scriptures encourage our final thoughts of the day to turn heavenward. The apostle Paul and Silas were thrown into prison and Acts records, "Around *midnight,* Paul and Silas were praying and singing hymns to God, and the other prisoners were listening." (Acts 16:25, NLT)

Also in the New Testament, we see the model of Jesus in relation to prayer at night. "Afterward [Jesus] went up into the hills by himself to pray. *Night fell* while he was there alone." (Matthew 14:23, NLT) Jesus was in constant communication with God and after he spent his appointed time in prayer, a great ministry followed. *Prayerlessness* always equals *powerlessness*.

True prayer requires a daily discipline, commitment and focus. Observe how Jesus Christ finished his earthly life with a strong commitment to prayer. As the prophet Jeremiah wrote, "You will search for me. And when you search for me with all your heart, you will find me!" (Jeremiah 29:13, NCV)

WHERE TO PRAY

Talking about a location for prayer, Jesus told his disciples, "When you pray, you should go into your room and close the door and pray to your Father who cannot be seen. Your Father can see what is done in secret, and he will reward you." (Matthew 6:6) In some translations the word "room" becomes "closet." Jesus was telling his followers not to pray for show but to be different from the Pharisees. These religious leaders loved to pray vain and repetitious prayers in the open and for the majority of the time in front of other people in public.

The disciples instantly recognized that Jesus was not praying according to the tradition of the day or in the temple. To the contrary, Jesus prayed everywhere and indicated that prayer was not limited to a particular locality or ritual. Jesus taught the masses that intimacy and a relationship with the Heavenly Father was the key to fulfilled prayer.

Jesus prayed in isolation. "After sending [the disciples] away, [Jesus] went into the hills to pray." (Mark 6:46, NCV) The members of the early Church prayed near the riverside. "On the Sabbath day we went outside the city gate to the river where we thought we would find a special place for prayer. Some women had gathered there, so we sat down and talked with them." (Acts

16:13, NCV) Other times, Jesus and his disciples prayed on a mountainside. "About eight days later Jesus took Peter, James, and John to a mountain to pray." (Luke 9:28, NLT)

The location is unimportant but you need to find a place to meet regularly with the Lord and pray. Select a place where you feel comfortable praying. The important aspect is that you have peace and a level of comfort in a particular place. It doesn't have to be in a church or a religious setting. You could pray while driving to the office or in your favorite chair in the living room. You may have to designate a special place in your home for prayer.

My good friend, Dr. Dick Eastman, has a unique place in his home called "the Gap." He enters this special room as a place to go and commune with God where he prays for the nations of the world. It's a great idea that possibly you should consider. As you pray, the Holy Spirit will assist and direct you to the best place for you to pray.

VARIOUS POSTURES FOR PRAYER

The ultimate purpose of true prayer is to communicate and deepen our relationship with our Heavenly Father. As a man, Jesus prayed in numerous positions and styles during his constant communion with the Father. However, from the Bible we gather that a majority of the prayers of Jesus were in isolated places (sitting and kneeling alone).

There are three most common postures for prayer.

Kneeling: "When Solomon finished making these prayers and requests to the Lord, he stood up in front of the altar of the Lord, where he had been *kneeling* with his hands raised toward heaven." (1 Kings 8:54, NLT)

Sitting: "Then King David went in and *sat* before the Lord and prayed, "Who am I, O Lord God, and what is my family, that you have brought me this far?" (1 Chronicles 17:16, NLT)

14

Standing: "And whenever you *stand* praying, if you have anything against anyone, forgive him, that your Father in heaven may also forgive you your trespasses." (Mark 11:25, NKJV)

"And the tax collector, *standing* afar off, would not so much as raise his eyes to heaven, but beat his breast, saying, 'God, be merciful to me a sinner!' " (Luke 18:13, NKJV)

Proclamation Forms of Prayer

Walking: "Elisha got up and *walked back and forth* in the room a few times. Then he stretched himself out again on the child. This time the boy sneezed seven times and opened his eyes!" (2 Kings 4:35, NLT)

Hands raised: "So wherever you assemble, I want men to pray *with holy hands lifted up* to God, free from anger and controversy." (1 Timothy 2:8, NLT)

Consecrated Forms of Praying

Lying down: "[Jesus] went on a little farther and *fell face down* on the ground. He prayed that, if it were possible, the awful hour awaiting him might pass him by." (Mark 14:35, NLT)

Bowing: "So Moses made haste and *bowed his head* toward the earth, and worshiped." (Exodus 34:8, NKJV)

As a man of prayer, we ask the Lord to teach us to pray. It is interesting to underscore that the disciples who lived with Jesus for three and a half years, never asked the Master to teach them how to preach or heal the sick. Instead, these disciples asked Jesus to teach them how to pray. Why prayer? They had come to recognize that it was the prayer life of Jesus with his Heavenly Father where Jesus drew his supernatural power on Earth.

The classic day when Jesus taught his disciples about prayer came during the Sermon on the Mount. (Matthew 6:9–13 and Luke 11:2–4, NLT) We commonly call this prayer "the Lord's Prayer." If you study the original Greek language for this familiar passage, you understand the true meaning of the phrase in Luke 11:2 (NLT) "This is how you should pray . . ." is closer to "to pray in this manner or style or pattern."

We are not to take the Lord's Prayer as vain repetition because Jesus warned his disciples not to use vain repetition for prayer or empty words which are not heart felt. Here is the text of the Lord's Prayer

> "In this manner, therefore, pray: Our Father in heaven, Hallowed be Your name. Your kingdom come. Your will be done On earth as it is in heaven. Give us this day our daily bread. And forgive us our debts, As we forgive our debtors. And do not lead us into temptation, But deliver us from the evil one. For Yours is the kingdom and the power and the glory forever. Amen." (Matthew 6:9–13, NKJV)

If we take this prayer as a model and break it down by verse, we could easily develop a deeper understanding of its meaning and promise.

Jesus began his prayer with adoration or praise (Matthew 6:9)—"In this manner, therefore, pray: Our Father in heaven, Hallowed be Your name." Jesus recognized his relationship with the Heavenly Father.

Matthew 6:10—"Your kingdom come. Your will be done On earth as it is in heaven." Jesus was emphasizing the importance of knowing God and praying God's will back to him.

Matthew 6:11—"Give us this day our daily bread." Jesus wanted us to ask our Heavenly Father for the daily provision of our needs—physical, emotional, and spiritual.

Matthew 6:12—"And forgive us our debts, As we forgive our debtors." This part of the prayer is a deliberate time to ask for forgiveness and to release others who have wronged us.

Matthew 6:13a—Now the prayer turns into a prayer for protection, saying, "And do not lead us into temptation, But deliver us from the evil one." We need to ask God to protect us from evil and the influences of evil.

Finally, the prayer ends with praise and worship in Matthew 6:13b—"For Yours is the kingdom and the power and the glory forever. Amen." The prayer concludes essentially saying, "Here we are giving back to God, by concluding in an expectant heart which is full of praise and worship." Throughout the Psalms, a section is ended with the word "selah," which means "pause and think about it." So this passage from Jesus ends with the word "Amen," or "May it be so."

From this chapter, you can see there is no exacting formula for prayer. You can pray over lunch, in the car on the way home, before a meeting, or at night before you retire with your wife. The key to becoming a man of prayer is to become a praying man. The remainder of this book gives examples and additional Bible references so you can begin this exciting journey of faith. With these model prayers, you can pray through the book from cover to cover or use the table of contents for a particular situation from your life.

Let's pray.

PRAYERS

for

VARIOUS NEEDS

CHAPTER 3

Prayers for the Morning

⬦

A STORY ABOUT MORNING PRAYER

The clock radio breaks into Paul's day. He turns over and hits the snooze button. It's too early in the morning—especially for prayer. Instead of the silence of the morning, Paul tries to fill his day with noise—from a television set or something. He is uncomfortable without constant noise. His day is full of constant activity—on the telephone or preparing for an appointment. If there is any lag in the day, Paul is at loose ends and doesn't know what to do with himself.

Solitude is something many people avoid. As Bill Watkins writes in *The Busy Christian's Guide to Experiencing God More*, "Some professionals I have worked with never travel alone, eat alone, or spend much time alone in their office. They seem to need an entourage around them just about all of the time. . . . They are desperately needy people, and one of the ways they show it is by avoiding solitude."

Early in the morning is an ideal time to turn to God in prayer and solitude. When Jesus walked the face of the earth and began his ministry, the crowds rushed to him. They carried their sick so they could be touched and healed; people sat around listening to Jesus tell stories and teach. The early chapters of the Gospel of Mark tell us about one of the busiest days for Jesus. He touched and healed people late into the night. Early the next morning, his disciples looked for Jesus and couldn't locate their Master. Finally they found Jesus alone on a hillside in prayer. "Lord, people are looking for you," they said to him.

Jesus wasn't concerned that he had been missed. For the first concern of his day, Jesus wanted to talk with his Heavenly Father. Prayer in the morning was more important than interaction with people.

Prayers in the morning don't have to be lengthy but are an excellent way to start a day of activity. Pastor Jack Hayford encourages men to kneel as their first step out of bed in the morning. The act of kneeling gives a humble beginning to the day and simply tells our Heavenly Father, "God, the day is yours. My life is yours. Take this day and walk with me." The following prayers will give you some direction for morning prayers.

Let's pray:

⌑

Prayer for Strength for the Morning

God, I need your strength for the activities of today. Sometimes in the rush of life, it's all I can do to climb out of bed and into a new day. With your mighty hand, strengthen my legs to walk and strengthen my arms to serve you. As your presence fills my life, help me to have a sense of how you fill my life with strength for what is ahead.

I know that you are with me, God, and I ask that I will not become dismayed with any situation which I may face today. Instead I want to walk in your divine strength and power that only you can give. Thank you in advance for your provision and strength. I want to acknowledge my dependence on you.

Amen.

⊗

Prayer for Commitment of Today's Plans

God, if you open my appointment book, you'll see that I've made a few plans for today. There are some meetings scheduled, some phone calls to make and some plans which have been made. I want to turn these plans over into your capable hands.

Lord, please make these plans agreeable with your will for my day. As my plans are in alignment with your will and desires, I know I will be successful in my day. God, direct my plans and make them your plans.

Thank you, Father, for the Holy Spirit which abides in me and guides me according to your plans for my life. Help me to be a man who does what I should do and to stay focused on that commitment. Thank you for giving me the faith to trust you for solutions to today's difficulties and problems. As I commit these plans to you, I ask for flexibility and a constant awareness of your presence in my day.

Amen.

⊗

Prayer for Guidance

God, this morning, I ask that you guide the steps that I take. As a man, help me to walk in a manner worthy of you and your will. I ask for your guidance for every situation and circumstance which comes into my life. Teach me to number my days according to your wisdom and I ask you to fill me with the knowledge of your will for my life today.

Thank you, Heavenly Father, that your wisdom and guidance is different than that of the world. The wisdom of the world looks at the majority then follows in the footsteps of peers. Instead, Lord, I want to follow your guidance and instruction from the Bible for my life. Sometimes such steps go directly contrary to the world around me. For example, the world says, "It's just one little white lie." Instead, the Bible tells us to value truth and not to shade it. Help me to follow you in every area of today. Guide me in the path of righteousness for your namesake.

Amen.

⊠

Prayer to Avoid the Traps of Temptation

This morning, God, I give my day to you. I don't know what the details of today will hold but I pray that you will help me avoid the traps of temptation. The Bible says that you are faithful in my life and you will not permit me to be tempted beyond what I am able to bear. In the middle of every temptation, Heavenly Father, you provide the way of escape. Sometimes that way is simply fleeing. Other times, I need to turn my thoughts toward heaven and Scripture instead of turning them toward myself.

I ask, Lord, that you would keep me sober and vigilant in the day ahead. Guide my steps and protect them so I don't stumble and fall flat on my face. This morning, I ask you to place a protective hedge around myself, my family, and my loved ones—no matter where they are.

Amen.

⌖

BIBLE VERSES ABOUT PRAYER IN THE MORNING

So one night the king of Aram sent a great army with many chariots and horses to surround the city. When the servant of the man of God got up *early the next morning* and went outside, there were troops, horses, and chariots everywhere. 'Ah, my lord, what will we do now?" he cried out to Elisha.

"Don't be afraid!" Elisha told him. "For there are more on our side than on theirs!"

Then Elisha prayed—"O Lord, open his eyes and let him see!" The Lord opened his servant's eyes, and when Elisha looked up, he saw that the hillside around him was filled with horses and chariots of fire. As the Aramean army advanced toward them, Elisha prayed, "O Lord, please make them blind." And the Lord did as Elisha asked. (2 Kings 6:14–18, NLT)

That evening, after the sun went down, the people brought to Jesus all who were sick and had demons in them. The whole town gathered at the door. Jesus healed many who had different kinds of sicknesses, and he forced many demons to leave people. But he would not allow the demons to speak, because they knew who he was.

Early the next morning, while it was still dark, Jesus woke and left the house. He went to a lonely place, where he prayed. Simon and his friends went to look for Jesus. When they found him, they said, "Everyone is looking for you!"

Jesus answered, "We should go to other towns around here so I can preach there too. That is the reason I came." (Mark 1:32–38, NCV)

CHAPTER 4

Prayers at Noon

⬦

A Story About Prayer at Noon

In postwar Germany, almost four hundred men served in the air wing, but these soldiers had almost no desire for anything religious. The young chaplain assigned to the wing felt a sense of failure and discouragement. After a low turnout to a chapel service, he decided to skip lunch and spend his noon hour in prayer. In despair, he walked to a nearby forest and fell to his knees near an old stump.

The chaplain poured out his heart to God and asked what to do next. Then the chaplain spent time listening and seemed to hear God speak to his heart: "Go to the base store where the men are and I will show you what to do." Obedient to the voice of God, the next day, the chaplain went to the base store or the PX.

As he walked into the room, a large puff of smoke rolled out the door and he noticed the loud conversation and the smell of stale beer. Across the milling crowd, the chaplain spied a young pilot with a letter in his hand and sitting in the corner. He had a look of despair across his face. "Go and sit by that man," God's voice seemed to say, and the chaplain walked over to the table and sat down.

For a long while, the pilot said nothing, then he handed the letter to the chaplain. The words told the story: his wife wanted a divorce; she had met another man and was tired of waiting for her pilot husband.

The chaplain began to tell the pilot about his own grief—the small audiences, his own feelings of despair, and how he went at noon to the stump and prayed, then came to the PX.

When the chaplain came to the end of his story, the young pilot had tears in his eyes. "I guess that's the way I feel, too, only I feel like a failure as a man and a husband. Why don't we go out to that old stump today at noon? As we pray together, possibly we both will discover what to do next."

The two men kneeled in the forest. Through prayer, the pilot felt encouraged and the chaplain asked the young man to return to his office in the morning.

To the chaplain's surprise, the next day, the man showed up with two friends in tow; both men were looking for fresh answers to personal pain. Two mornings later the number of men had increased to eight. By the end of the week, so many soldiers crowded into the tiny office that they needed to find a larger meeting place. Three weeks later, three hundred men attended the chaplain's service of Holy Communion. The reputation of the air wing spread and became famous across Europe for their dynamic Christian men. These changes started from one sincere man praying at noon and show the startling power of prayer.

Let's pray:

◇

Prayer at Noon for Unmet Expectations

God, a number of things have happened today unex-pectedly. I planned for the day to go one way and it has been taken in a totally different direction. Help me to release my expectations for the day and for other peo-ple. I want to release these expectations to you and help me to wait on you to fulfill your wishes and your word. You alone will become my expectation and grant me to hold fast to the confession of my hope without wavering. Thank you that you have promised to be faithful.

Amen.

◇

Prayer at Noon for Confidence

Dear Lord, you said that in quietness and confidence our strength would be found. I pray that I will not throw away my confidence and instead realize that my confidence is a just reward. Help me to have the endur-ance that I need so that I can do your will then receive your promise. Fill my life and heart with confidence of the sort that only you can provide.

Amen.

◇

Prayer at Noon Against Adversity

Lord, some days it seems like trouble surrounds me. To-day is one of those days and I pray God that you would comfort me in my adversity. I pray that all things will work together for good because I am called according to your purpose. As I continue moving ahead with my life in the middle of this adversity, I pray that you, God, will revive me. I ask that you will stretch out your hand against the wrath from my enemies and that your right hand would save me.

Amen.

⊠

Prayer at Noon for Unusual Stress

Almighty God, release me from the anxieties of this world. Help me to turn my cares over to you. You've said in your word that we should not be anxious about anything but *in everything* through prayer and supplication make our requests known to you. Thank you for the provision of a means of escape from the tensions that are overwhelming me. Help me to sense your presence and refreshing love.

Amen.

⊠

BIBLE VERSES FOR PRAYER AT NOON

Listen to my prayer, O God. Do not ignore my cry for help! Please listen and answer me, for I am overwhelmed by my troubles. My enemies shout at me, making loud and wicked threats. They bring trouble on me, hunting me down in their anger. My heart is in anguish. The terror of death overpowers me. Fear and trembling overwhelm me. I can't stop shaking.

Oh, how I wish I had wings like a dove; then I would fly away and rest! I would fly far away to the quiet of the wilderness. Interlude.

How quickly I would escape—far away from this wild storm of hatred. Destroy them, Lord, and confuse their speech, for I see violence and strife in the city. Its walls are patrolled day and night against invaders, but the real danger is wickedness within the city. Murder and robbery are everywhere there; threats and cheating are rampant in the streets.

It is not an enemy who taunts me—I could bear that. It is not my foes who so arrogantly insult me—I could have hidden from them. Instead, it is you—my equal, my companion and close friend. What good fellowship we enjoyed as we walked together to the house of God.

Let death seize my enemies by surprise; let the grave swallow them alive, for evil makes its home within them. But I will call on God, and the Lord will rescue me.

Morning, *noon*, and night I plead aloud in my distress, and the Lord hears my voice. He rescues me and keeps me safe from the battle waged against me, even though many still oppose me. God, who is king forever, will hear me and will humble them. Interlude.

For my enemies refuse to change their ways; they do not fear God. (Psalm 55:1–19, NLT)

The next day as Cornelius's messengers were nearing the city, Peter went up to the flat roof to pray. It was about *noon*, and he was hungry. But while lunch was being prepared, he fell into a trance. He saw the sky open, and something like a large sheet was let down by its four corners. In the sheet were all sorts of animals, reptiles, and birds. Then a voice said to him, "Get up, Peter; kill and eat them."

"Never, Lord," Peter declared. "I have never in all my life eaten anything forbidden by our Jewish laws."

The voice spoke again, "If God says something is acceptable, don't say it isn't." The same vision was repeated three times. Then the sheet was pulled up again to heaven. Peter was very perplexed. What could the vision mean? Just then the men sent by Cornelius found the house and stood outside at the gate. They asked if this was the place where Simon Peter was staying.

Meanwhile, as Peter was puzzling over the vision, the Holy Spirit said to him, "Three men have come looking for you. Go down and go with them without hesitation. All is well, for I have sent them."

So Peter went down and said, "I'm the man you are looking for. Why have you come?"

They said, "We were sent by Cornelius, a Roman officer. He is a devout man who fears the God of Israel and is well respected by all the Jews. A holy angel instructed him to send for you so you can go to his house and give him a message." (Acts 10:9–22, NLT)

Paul said, "Friends, fellow Jews, listen to my defense to you."

When the Jews heard him speaking the Jewish language, they became very quiet. Paul said, "I am a Jew, born in Tarsus in the country of Cilicia, but I grew up in this city. I was a student of Gamaliel, who carefully taught me everything about the law of our ancestors. I was very serious about serving God, just as are all of you here today.

"I persecuted the people who followed the Way of Jesus, and some of them were even killed. I arrested men and women and put them in jail. The high priest and the whole council of older Jewish leaders can tell you this is true. They gave me letters to the Jewish brothers in Damascus. So I was going there to arrest these people and bring them back to Jerusalem to be punished.

"About *noon* when I came near Damascus, a bright light from heaven suddenly flashed all around me. I fell to the ground and heard a voice saying, 'Saul, Saul, why are you persecuting me?'

"I asked, 'Who are you, Lord?' The voice said, 'I am Jesus from Nazareth whom you are persecuting.'

"Those who were with me did not hear the voice, but they saw the light." (Acts 22:1–9, NCV)

CHAPTER 5

Prayers in the Night

⊠

A Story About Prayer in the Night

All of his life, Dino Andreadis dreamed of being a movie star. From Montreal, Dino made his way to Hollywood and pounded on doors, trying to get a part in the film or television industry. Just when his agent was beginning to find opportunities for work, Dino was informed by the Immigration and Naturalization Service that as a Canadian he could not work without an American green card. There were two alternatives—pay $5,000 for a green card or marry an American.

Since he was short on cash, Dino began to search the nightclubs and he found a beautiful young woman who was willing to marry him. Energized, he rushed home to make plans. On the bus to Montreal, a man slipped a printed message into his hand: *Jesus Christ is coming soon!*

Suddenly Dino was confused and decided to get off at the next bus stop—the wrong one. There stood David, the man who had given Dino the tract, and he took the opportunity to share the Good News About Jesus with Dino.

The next morning, a woman came to Dino's door. She was a friend of David's. "I felt compelled to pray for you all night," she said. "Whatever it is you are about to do, don't do it!" Then she left.

The words shocked Dino into action. He called off the marriage and asked Christ into his life. The change of direction guided him from acting into a worldwide evangelistic ministry. With his music, Dino has touched millions.

As you pray in the evening or the night, remember the diligence and commitment of this woman of prayer. It may change the way you pray in the evening.

Let's pray:

◇

Prayers for Sleep and Safety

Heavenly Father, first, I want to thank you for today. It's been full of a variety of activities whether with my family or work. My conversation and actions from today have not been perfect. I admit that I've failed to meet the expectations of others and even myself. Please forgive me for these failures. I ask for your strength and peace to fill my life.

Lord, sometimes it's difficult to put off my thoughts and plans till tomorrow. Like a late-night movie, these images play in my mind with different endings. I ask you to take these situations for tomorrow. I give them into your hands and ask for you to give me the rest which I need for tonight. You say in the Bible that you give your beloved sleep. I ask you to fill my dreams and thoughts with your presence. Help me to sleep in peace.

God, I pray for my immediate family. Please watch over them tonight as I sleep. Keep them in the palm of your hand. In the Bible you say that your thoughts of us are greater than the grains of sand in the desert. I ask that through your mighty power, you will protect and guard my family through tonight. I love you, God. Help me to express that love to you every day and to love my family.

Amen.

⟡

Prayers for When You Can't Rest

Lord, for some strange reason, I can't sleep tonight. It could be the burdens of today or life in general. There are more problems to be solved and more relationships to heal, but I know I will not be effective tomorrow without some rest.

In the New Testament, Jesus said, "Come to me all you who are weary and burdened, and I will give you rest. Take my yoke upon you and learn from me, for I am gentle and humble in heart, and you will find rest for your souls. For my yoke is easy and my burden is light." (Matthew 11:28–30, NIV) Sometimes the burdens of this life are more than I can easily bear, Lord. So I ask for your help and involvement in these burdens. Please take them from my shoulders and replace them with something which I can carry.

I acknowledge that I will not be able to resolve all of my difficulties tonight. Some situations take time to heal and time for resolution. Instead, I admit that I give up and turn these situations into the capable hands of my Heavenly Father. You take these problems and fill my thoughts and life with peace. Give me the rest which I need for this evening.

Amen.

⊠

Prayer for the Things We Can't See

Lord, your world is covered with darkness right now. If the electricity was turned off, it would be very black. In the night, my thoughts and actions sometimes fall black. I think thoughts I shouldn't think, and in fact, I do things that I shouldn't do.

Help me to be more keenly aware of your presence and guidance in my life. The Psalmist told us, "When I rise up, you are there. When I lay down to sleep, you are there. If I go up to heaven, you are there and if I descend into hell, you are there." Your presence is always here—whether I am conscious of it or not.

Heavenly Father, I want to know you more tonight. I want to sense your intimate love and involvement in my daily life. I kneel before you this evening and want to talk with you about things I can't see in my tomorrow and my future. Just as blackness covers the earth in the evening, so a black curtain hangs over my vision for what tomorrow will hold, and in fact, all of my tomorrows will hold. As the ruler of heaven and earth, God, you see both sides of the curtain. You see today and what has happened, yet you also see tomorrow.

I want to turn those unseen actions and thoughts over into your capable hands. I ask you to take each action for tomorrow and use it for the Glory of your kingdom—here on earth and in heaven. Tonight I thank you that you are all-seeing and all-knowing—even in the darkness of evening.

Amen.

⊠

Bible Verses About Prayer in the Evening

Rise during the *night* and cry out. Pour out your hearts like water to the Lord. Lift up your hands to him in prayer. Plead for your children as they faint with hunger in the streets. (Lam 2:19, NLT)

O Lord, I am calling to you. Please hurry! Listen when I cry to you for help! Accept my prayer as incense offered to you, and my upraised hands as an *evening* offering. Take control of what I say, O Lord, and keep my lips sealed. Don't let me lust for evil things; don't let me participate in acts of wickedness. Don't let me share in the delicacies of those who do evil. Let the godly strike me! It will be a kindness! If they reprove me, it is soothing medicine. Don't let me refuse it. But I am in constant prayer against the wicked and their deeds. When their leaders are thrown down from a cliff, they will listen to my words and find them pleasing.

Even as a farmer breaks up the soil and brings up rocks, so the bones of the wicked will be scattered without a decent burial. I look to you for help, O Sovereign Lord. You are my refuge; don't let them kill me. Keep me out of the traps they have set for me, out of the snares of those who do evil. Let the wicked fall into their own snares, but let me escape. (Psalm 141:1–10, NLT)

Those who live in the shelter of the Most High will find rest in the shadow of the Almighty. This I declare of the Lord: He alone is my refuge, my place of safety; he is my God, and I am trusting him. For he will rescue you from every trap and protect you from the fatal plague. He will shield you with his wings. He will shelter you with his feathers. His faithful promises are your armor and protection.

Do not be afraid of the terrors of the *night*, nor fear the dangers of the day, nor dread the plague that stalks in darkness, nor the disaster that strikes at midday. Though a thousand fall at your side, though ten thousand are dying around you, these evils will not touch you. But you will see it with your eyes; you will see how the wicked are punished.

If you make the Lord your refuge, if you make the Most High your shelter, no evil will conquer you; no plague will come near your dwelling. For he orders his angels to protect you wherever you go. They will hold you with their hands to keep you from striking your foot on a stone. You will trample down lions and poisonous snakes; you will crush fierce lions and serpents under your feet! (Psalm 91:1–13, NLT)

But don't be afraid of those who threaten you. For the time is coming when everything will be revealed; all that is secret will be made public. What I tell you now in the *darkness*, shout abroad when daybreak comes. What I whisper in your ears, shout from the housetops for all to hear!

Don't be afraid of those who want to kill you. They can only kill your body; they cannot touch your soul. Fear only God, who can destroy both soul and body in hell. Not even a sparrow, worth only half a penny, can fall to the ground without your Father knowing it. And the very hairs on your head are all numbered.

So don't be afraid; you are more valuable to him than a whole flock of sparrows. "If anyone acknowledges me publicly here on earth, I will openly acknowledge that person before my Father in heaven." (Matthew 10:26–32, NLT)

CHAPTER 6

Prayers for the Workplace

⊠

A STORY ABOUT WORK

Gordon MacDonald felt a desperate need for a restored spiritual passion and direction from God with his work. He was on an airplane and headed for a meeting which would determine the direction of his work. His passion was missing and with good reason. MacDonald felt a deep resentment toward a colleague.

For many days, Gordon tried to get rid of his vindictive thoughts toward this coworker. No matter how he tried, thoughts flooded his mind during the night with means to pay his colleague back. MacDonald wanted to embarrass him and damage his credibility in front of his peers. His thoughts about the colleague consumed him to the point where it dominated him. During this plane trip, he suddenly realized that he had sunk to a low level in that relationship which was spilling over into his entire life. It was a vicious circle that he wanted to escape.

MacDonald writes about his transformation in *Restoring Your Spiritual Passion*, saying, "As the plane entered the landing pattern,

I found myself crying silently to God for power both to forgive and to experience liberation from my poisoned spirit. Suddenly it was as if an invisible knife cut a hole in my chest, and I literally felt a thick substance oozing from within. Moments later I felt as if I'd been flushed out. I'd lost negative spiritual weight, the kind I needed to lose: I was free. I fairly bounced off that plane and soon entered a meeting that did in fact change the direction of my entire life."

It's unclear the specifics of MacDonald's situation but it's un-important because each of us encounters conflict in our workplace. It's a natural part of being a man in today's world. Our indepen-dent nature smashes against someone in authority. Or a terrific idea gets ignored and you are forced to execute an inferior idea which eventually flops. Or maybe your personality doesn't mesh with the person at the next desk and you are forced to work with that person day in and day out—sometimes in close range. Or possibly your supervisor is making your life miserable and handing you all of the dreg assignments.

In whatever situation you face, it's good to know that you are in touch with the King of Kings. We learn in the Psalms that God directs the rivers *and* the heart of the king. The Lord can also direct you, your coworkers, your supervisor, and the other leaders in your workplace. As we talk with God about our struggles and difficulties, his power and wisdom can flow into the situation. It is only available if we ask through prayer.

Let's pray:

◇

Prayer for Your Supervisor(s)

God, today I want to pray for the leadership in my company. I pray for their day and the activities of this day, their relationships and decisions. I pray they will experience your blessings today.

I ask that you will be their strength, confidence, and courage. I pray that they will be imitators of you today and exercise love, truth, and the light of your wisdom inside our office.

Amen.

⊠

Prayer for Your Diligence with Work

God, you said in the Bible that if a man is diligent in his business, then he will stand before kings and not stand before mean men. Today, help me to diligently give every area of my work to you. Allow my talents and my gifts to be stirred up and used today. Help me to obey you in all things, not only through my service to others but in a singleness of heart which is devoted to you. Let my hands be strong and not weak so that you will reward my work. For the Bible says that the diligent will be fat. I ask you to bless the work of my hands today.

Amen.

⊠

Prayer for Your Coworkers

Heavenly Father, I pray a special blessing on my coworkers, the members of my staff and every person who enters the door of our company. Help every individual to sense your goodness, mercy, and grace from our company.

I ask for your Holy Spirit to go before us today and prepare the way for our daily activities. Lord, work in us and through us today to accomplish your will and plans for our business. We want to glorify you and your intimate involvement in our everyday activities and lives.

Thank you for hearing my prayer.
Amen.

⊠

Prayer for Anyone Encountered Through Your Work

Father God, today I want to pray for the people who will cross my path through my work. I ask for you to help me encourage these people to know and follow you—not in an offensive way but in a way which will honor your name and please you. Teach me how to build up other people and to bear their weaknesses instead of pleasing myself. I want to encourage others not for a selfish motive but simply for their own good. Let me show others how to rejoice in you and your actions in my life—despite any tribulations or difficulties that I may be going through. Help me to share your peace with others so that each person is built up in their faith. Prompt me, God, and enable me to speak an appropriate word in season so that others may be comforted.

Amen.

⊠

Prayer for Myself in a Difficulty at Work

God, I'm mad and upset about my work situation. It's hard to work with ———— and ————. Why did you bring him to the company in the first place? Why did you bring me to this company?

First, I want to thank you for helping me keep my anger in check. You say in Proverbs that a fool gives full vent to his anger but a wise man keeps himself under

44

control. I want to be like that wise man and not the fool. Give me peace in the middle of the conflict at work.

Lord, if I'm honest, I want you to change ———. Work in his life and heart. Help him to see my viewpoint and help us to resolve this difficult situation.

At the same time, I know that I can never change another person. I can't actually crawl inside his skin then move and act in his way. There is only one person I *can* change—and that is me. I ask that you would turn the light of honesty and truth on my own life and heart. Through that light, shine into the dark and hidden places of my life. Show me how I can change, then motivate me to make those changes. I don't want to act or live in my own strength but ask that your mighty power would live in my life today so that I can be a man who is known as a man who is living for you.

Amen.

◇

Prayer for a Difficult Coworker Relationship

Lord, this prayer is hard. I don't want to be praying for ———. He works in my office and ——— is causing a lot of difficulty. You know all of the specifics and I thank you that you know the beginning and the ending of every situation in life. Whether we acknowledge it or not, you are in control of the universe.

Today, I pray that you will reach out through your divine spirit and touch the life of ———. Help him to understand the difficulty that we now face. Motivate him and guide him to be willing to resolve this conflict. I pray you would soften his heart so ——— is willing to do his part to change the situation.

Lord, we need a creative idea. I pray you would give me something that hasn't been considered or thought about for this situation. Blow a fresh wind of change and inspiration into the conflict and work situation. Help me not to be stalled with conflict and instead help peace to reign in this situation.

Forgive me, Heavenly Father, for wrong thoughts and harshly spoken words. Forgive these words which have come from my mouth as well as the words from ———. Give me an ability that I don't have on my own strength—the ability to love and respect ———.

Whether you bring the answer to this situation today or tomorrow or next month or next year, help me to be faithful in talking with you about it and asking for your continued guidance. I want to thank you in advance for the resolution to this difficulty. It may not be in the way I plan or the way anyone could have planned. I ask for your plan and resolution.

Amen.

⊠

Prayer for My Supervisor in a Difficult Situation

Heavenly Father, in your Word, you've told us that we should be subjected one to another. I thank you that you have put ——— as a supervisor and director for my work and occupation. While your name doesn't appear on any organization charts, I want to acknowledge that you are the director and true leader of the world. I ask you to be the boss in my life—for every thought, every action and every word—spoken or unspoken.

Today, I want to pray for ———. Help him to make wise decisions. Guide his physical steps and his actions.

Whether he knows you personally or not, lead him in the way of righteousness.

I want to be available for you, Lord. I give my own life into your capable hands and ask for you to guide my words and steps. If you want to use me as an instrument of your peace in the life of my supervisor ———, then I pray you will give me the right circumstance and the correct boldness to talk about you.

Thank you that you have the large picture of my life—throughout every minute of every day. Bless and prosper ———.

Amen.

◇

Prayer for Healing in the Workplace

Father, thank you for the provision of my place to work. In my heart, I may not feel too thankful because of the difficulties there—nonetheless, with my mind, I want to thank you. It's not easy for people to work together at a task—any task. We read about the difficulties that the disciples of Jesus had when they were together.

The Bible tells the story about Jesus and the disciples walking down the road. Jesus turned and asked them what they were discussing. The disciples hedged, Lord, from an answer because they had been arguing about who would be the greatest in your kingdom. Isn't that just like mankind, Lord? We all want to be the top dog in our particular place of business.

Lord, I want a new sense of humility in my workplace. Help me to be a peacemaker in the midst of arguments and strife. Jesus told us, "Blessed are the peacemakers for they shall see God." Help me to be the peacemaker and give me that spiritual insight into an earthly situation. If the answer doesn't come immediately, then please give me the strength and patience to wait on you for the answer.

I want to thank you in advance for your intimate care and concern about every detail of our lives.

Amen.

◇

BIBLE VERSES ABOUT WORK

Some Pharisees saw them do it and protested, "Your disciples shouldn't be doing that! It's against the law to *work* by harvesting grain on the Sabbath."

But Jesus said to them, "Haven't you ever read in the Scriptures what King David did when he and his companions were hungry? He went into the house of God, and they ate the special bread reserved for the priests alone. That was breaking the law, too.

"And haven't you ever read in the law of Moses that the priests on duty in the Temple may work on the Sabbath?

"I tell you, there is one here who is even greater than the Temple! But you would not have condemned those who aren't guilty if you knew the meaning of this Scripture: 'I want you to be merciful; I don't want your sacrifices.' For I, the Son of Man, am master even of the Sabbath."

Then he went over to the synagogue, where he noticed a man with a deformed hand. The Pharisees asked Jesus, "Is it legal to work by healing on the Sabbath day?" (They were, of course, hoping he would say yes, so they could bring charges against him.)

And he answered, "If you had one sheep, and it fell into a well on the Sabbath, wouldn't you get to work and pull it out? Of course you would. And how much more valuable is a person than a sheep! Yes, it is right to do good on the Sabbath."

Then he said to the man, "Reach out your hand." The man reached out his hand, and it became normal, just like the other one. Then the Pharisees called a meeting and discussed plans for killing Jesus. But Jesus knew what they were planning. He left that area, and many people followed him. He healed all the sick among them, but he warned them not to say who he was. (Matthew 12:2–16, NLT)

Work hard, but not just to please your masters when they are watching. As slaves of Christ, do the will of God with all your heart. Work with enthusiasm, as though you were working for the Lord rather than for people.

Remember that the Lord will reward each one of us for the good we do, whether we are slaves or free. And in the same way, you masters must treat your slaves right. Don't threaten them; remember, you both have the same Master in heaven, and he has no favorites.

A final word: Be strong with the Lord's mighty power. Put on all of God's armor so that you will be able to stand firm against all strategies and tricks of the Devil. For we are not fighting against people made of flesh and blood, but against the evil rulers and authorities of the unseen world, against those mighty powers of darkness who rule this world, and against wicked spirits in the heavenly realms. (Ephesians 6:6–12, NLT)

And now, dear brothers and sisters, we give you this command with the authority of our Lord Jesus Christ: Stay away from any Christian who lives in idleness and doesn't follow the tradition of hard *work* we gave you.

For you know that you ought to follow our example. We

were never lazy when we were with you. We never accepted food from anyone without paying for it. We worked hard day and night so that we would not be a burden to any of you. It wasn't that we didn't have the right to ask you to feed us, but we wanted to give you an example to follow. Even while we were with you, we gave you this rule: "Whoever does not *work* should not eat."

Yet we hear that some of you are living idle lives, refusing to work and wasting time meddling in other people's business. In the name of the Lord Jesus Christ, we appeal to such people—no, we command them: Settle down and get to work. Earn your own living. And I say to the rest of you, dear brothers and sisters, never get tired of doing good. (2 Thessalonians 3:6–13, NLT)

We use God's mighty weapons, not mere worldly weapons, to knock down the Devil's strongholds. With these weapons we break down every proud argument that keeps people from knowing God. With these weapons we conquer their rebellious ideas, and we teach them to obey Christ.

And we will punish those who remained disobedient after the rest of you became loyal and obedient. The trouble with you is that you make your decisions on the basis of appearance. You must recognize that we belong to Christ just as much as those who proudly declare that they belong to Christ. (2 Corinthians 10:4–7, NLT)

CHAPTER 7

Prayers for Meals

◇

A STORY ABOUT PRAYER AT MEALS

According to Chuck Swindoll in *Growing Strong in the Seasons of Life*, much of what we first learned about prayer began around the kitchen table. He says, "From our earliest memory we've been programmed: If you don't pray, you don't eat. It started with Pablum in the high chair, and it continues through porterhouse at the restaurant."

Chuck recounts three stages of mealtime prayers. The first stage was *snickering*, where his older brother and sister used the prayer time at meals for a laugh. Then the second stage followed, or *doubting* and cynicism about the importance of mealtime prayer. He felt, "This is a ritual—it serves no purpose—God knows I'm grateful." Such time at prayer for Chuck felt childish and needless. The third stage of mealtime prayers involves *preaching*, because you have a captive audience who has to listen to your prayers, then you use the time as a platform.

Instead of falling for one of these three stages, Chuck encourages families to follow several suggestions related to prayer at meals. First, think before you pray. Consider what sort of meal is on the table and what has transpired in your day, then pray about these matters. Or consider singing a table blessing for a change of pace. Or occasionally pray after the meal when your hunger pangs have ceased.

For the final check of your mealtime prayers, Chuck suggests, "When the meal is over and you get up to do the dishes, ask if anyone remembers what was prayed for. If they do, great. If they don't, sit back down at the table and ask why. You've got a lot more to be concerned about than a stack of dishes." Instead of falling into useless repetition about mealtime, let's look for some fresh ways to ask God's blessing on the food and our meal.

Let's pray:

⊠

Prayer for a Meal

Jesus, you said that you are the Bread of Life. I know that through you, I receive spiritual food and today I want to thank you for this physical food. I thank you, God, that you have provided this food and that I don't have to worry about what I will be eating. I pray that you will continue to help me grow in my ability to trust you— in all things. I know that true joy and blessing come from you and I'm trusting you with all of my heart.

Amen.

⊠

Prayer of Thanksgiving for God's Provision

God, I want to thank you for this meal. Everything that I have—my life, my possessions, and this food— comes from your gracious provision.

Thank you, Lord, that you care about the birds in the sky and the lilies of the field. The Bible explains how you've numbered the hairs on our head and I thank you that your thoughts about us are more numerous than the grains of sand. I give thanks, Father, for all that you have done through your son, Jesus Christ. He is the Good Shepherd of our lives. He is the light and the peace for all of our worries and concerns. I am thankful that you have given your promises and your guidance in the Bible. Lord, I rejoice in the gift of life and how much you have given me. Thank you for providing us with substance to eat and with good health.

Right now I want to turn my thoughts to you in thanksgiving for this meal. I ask the food would nourish my body and give me strength to serve you in the hours and days ahead. Please bless the hands that prepared this meal. Thank you for your provision.

Amen.

⬦

Prayer of Consecration for Meals

Thank you, Father, for giving us this meal to eat. I ask you to cleanse and consecrate the food that we have received. Sanctify each person who is about to partake of this food. I thank you that this food is wholesome and will nourish our bodies. I praise you, God, for your abundant blessings.

Amen.

⬦

BIBLE VERSES ABOUT PRAYER FOR MEALS

So [Elijah] went to Zarephath. As he arrived at the gates of the city he saw a widow gathering sticks; and he asked her for a cup of water. As she was going to get it, he called to her, "Bring me a bite of bread too."

But she said, "I swear by the Lord your God that I haven't a single piece of bread in the house. And I have only a handful of flour left and a little cooking oil in the bottom of the jar. I was just gathering a few sticks to cook this last meal, and then my son and I must die of starvation."

But Elijah said to her, "Don't be afraid! Go ahead and cook that 'last meal,' but bake me a little loaf of bread first; and afterwards there will still be enough food for you and your son. For the Lord God of Israel says that there will always be plenty of flour and oil left in your containers until the time when the Lord sends rain and the crops grow again!"

So she did as Elijah said, and she and Elijah and her son continued to eat from her supply of flour and oil as long as it was needed. For no matter how much they used, there was always plenty left in the containers, just as the Lord had promised through Elijah! (1 Kings 17:10–16, TLB)

For the earth and every good thing in it belongs to the Lord and is yours to enjoy. If someone who isn't a Christian asks you out to dinner, go ahead; accept the invitation if you want to. Eat whatever is on the table and don't ask any questions about it. Then you won't know whether or not it has been used as a sacrifice to idols, and you won't risk having a bad conscience over eating it. But if someone warns you that this meat has been offered to idols, then don't eat it for the sake of the man who told you, and of his conscience.

In this case his feeling about it is the important thing, not yours. But why, you may ask, must I be guided and limited by what someone else thinks? If I can thank God for the food and enjoy it, why let someone spoil everything just because he thinks I am wrong?

Well, I'll tell you why. It is because you must do everything for the glory of God, even your eating and drinking. (1 Corinthians 10:26–31, TLB)

CHAPTER 8

Prayers with Your Wife

⊠

A STORY ABOUT WIVES

Musician John Fischer asks a question that many of us wonder in the rush of life—is it worth it? In *True Believers Don't Ask Why*, John recalls catching a 6 A.M. flight and wondering, "Shall I write about the emotional trauma my wife feels these days when I go on the road? Since she went back to work, I've been playing the role of Mr. Mom, *Father Knows Best*, and Garp, all rolled into one." As a Christian recording artist, author, and seminar leader, John often travels every weekend yet is home during the week. Recently his wife, Marti, returned to working full-time on a schedule where she's usually free on the weekends. The Fischers became like two ships passing in the night—not unlike many other couples.

Then John explains the mystery that is difficult to explain yet is something which resonates with every man: "After pouring twenty years into a career that I can't explain to the man on the street—a career without insurance, a pension plan, or retirement—

that I look in the mirror sometimes and wonder if it's worth it."

The delicate balance between home and career is a challenge for any husband. How do we love our wives and also provide for their physical, emotional, and spiritual needs? One of the methods of provision is prayer. Your job may require hours of travel or it may involve long hours at the office. You can encourage your wife through concerted and concentrated prayer. As you pray for your wife on a regular basis, it will strike a deep responsive chord in your soul and will transform the spiritual face of your family life.

Let's pray:

⊠

Prayer of Protection for Your Wife

God, you are my wife's refuge and strength, her very present help in trouble. I thank you, Lord, that she does not have to fear, because she dwells in the secret place of the Most High. Grant my wife to abide under your shadow and protective covering.

Heavenly Father, grant her your protection and permit no evil to enter her life or an accident to occur, not any plague or calamity to come near her. Give your angels special charge over her to accompany, defend, and preserve her in all her ways.

Thank you, Father, in Jesus' name.
Amen.

⊠

Prayer for Joy in Your Wife's Life

God, the Bible declares that a merry heart makes a cheerful countenance: but by sorrow of the heart the spirit is broken.

Today, I pray for my wife's joy. May her soul be joyful in you so that others will see the joy of the Lord in her face and life.

Restore in her life, the joy that comes from you. This joy is unspeakable and full of glory. Also fill my wife with your spiritual understanding. For you have said, blessed are the people that know the joyful sound, for they shall walk, O Lord, in the light of your presence.

In your name, I pray that my wife will rejoice all the day: and in your righteousness she will be lifted up.

Amen.

◇

Prayer When Your Wife is Emotionally Upset

A lmighty God, I pray for my wife that you would give her great peace. The Bible tells us that you are our peace and that you've broken down every wall. Sometimes, Lord, walls of emotion are instantly built inside us. Right now, my wife is upset and has built one of these walls. Through your power, I ask that you would tear down the wall and replace it with your love and peace.

Help her, Dear God, to think about things which are true, noble, just, pure, lovely, and are of a good report. Remove trouble from my wife and grant your salvation. Thank you, God, for your faithfulness to my wife.

Amen.

⊠

Prayer for Your Wife's Health

Gracious God, I want to pray today concerning my wife's health. As I pray this prayer, I believe your word and desire will be accomplished in my wife's life. In the Bible, you say, "Jesus took on our infirmities and bore our sickness." I pray therefore that my wife would walk in total and perfect health.

You, Lord, are the great physician and the one who heals. You are the one we can turn to for health and strength. Thank you for watching over my wife and allowing her to enjoy your blessing of health. I pray these words with confidence and faith in your answer which is exceedingly abundant above all I can ask or think.

Amen.

⊠

Pray for My Wife's Personal Growth

Lord, in the Bible, you tell us to rejoice in the wife of our youth. As I think about my wife, I want to first thank you for her presence in my life. Thank you for how you've brought —————— into my life and the powerful force that she brings each and every day.

Heavenly Father, you are the God who deals with the heart and touches our deep emotions. I ask for you to minister to my wife in a way that only your Spirit can help. I pray first, that you would help her to grow in her knowledge of the Bible. Awake in her life a desire to know you more and give her opportunities to develop the spiritual side of her life through Bible study as a group and on her own.

Then, God, I ask for you to touch the emotional nature of my wife. Reach your hand deep into her being and resolve any unmentioned issues. Help her to grow in her emotional relationship as a person. Increase my emotional relationship with ——— whom you have graciously given me as my wife. I look to you for provision of opportunities for ——— to improve the emotional side of her life. Give her opportunities to help and reach out to others and as a result grow as a person.

Finally, Lord, I thank you for my wife. Help me to celebrate the gifts and talents in her life. I want to be a blessing and encouragement to ———.

Amen.

Bible Verses About Wives

The man who finds a wife finds a treasure and receives favor from the Lord. (Proverbs 18:22, NLT)

Now about the questions you asked in your letter. Yes, it is good to live a celibate life. But because there is so much sexual immorality, each man should have his own wife, and each woman should have her own husband.

The husband should not deprive his wife of sexual intimacy, which is her right as a married woman, nor should the wife deprive her husband. The wife gives authority over her body to her husband, and the husband also gives authority over his body to his wife. So do not deprive each other of sexual relations. The only exception to this rule would be the agreement of both husband and wife to refrain from sexual intimacy for a limited time, so they can give themselves more completely to prayer. Afterward they should come together again so that Satan won't be able to tempt them because of their lack of self-control. This is only my suggestion. It's not meant to be an absolute rule. (1 Corinthians 7:1–6, NLT)

And you husbands must love your wives with the same love Christ showed the church. He gave up his life for her to make her holy and clean, washed by baptism and God's word. He did this to present her to himself as a glorious church without a spot or wrinkle or any other blemish. Instead, she will be holy and without fault.

In the same way, husbands ought to love their wives as they love their own bodies. For a man is actually loving himself when he loves his wife. No one hates his own body but lovingly cares for it, just as Christ cares for his body, which is the church. And we are his body.

As the Scriptures say, "A man leaves his father and mother and is joined to his wife, and the two are united into one." This is a great mystery, but it is an illustration of the way Christ and the church are one. So again I say, each man must love his wife as he loves himself, and the wife must respect her husband. (Ephesians 5:25–33, NLT)

CHAPTER 9

Prayers for Strife with Your Wife

◇

A Story About Marital Strife

One Saturday afternoon, Ron Wiseman was fixing his TV antenna on the roof in a rain storm; the main power line to the house had snapped and fell across the antenna. As Ron reached out, the current arced across his watch and knocked him unconscious. He rolled off the roof and bounced on his head off the concrete patio. The blow should have killed him instantly. Ron's wife, Betty, managed to drag him inside.

For nine years, the pastoral ministry had consumed Ron. "My home life was totally neglected, " Ron says. "Betty was a quiet, feeling person and highly emotional. I didn't know how to handle that. Rather than trying to handle the problem or seek Godly counsel, I avoided the situation and things worsened." To others, Ron appeared friendly, outgoing and loving. At home, Ron's violent outbursts caused Betty to retreat and withdraw even more. Betty felt like a phony as a pastor's wife. "We were like two strangers in the same house trying to kill each other. It was war," Ron says.

One Sunday evening in 1962 at church, Betty released her negative feelings to the Lord, "I asked God to show me how to be a loving wife and to cleanse me from negative feelings."

God's answer came through the accident. Now paralyzed from the neck down, Ron spent thirteen weeks in a hospital ICU. Eventually, Wiseman's condition remained severe yet stable. The doctor suggested Betty have life-support systems installed in their home. The third week of March Ron moved home. After he settled into the bedroom, Betty tiptoed in and gently touched Ron's cheek, his only area with feeling. "I shouted for her to get out and leave me to die," he recalls. Quietly Betty left the room.

In prayer, Ron asked God for healing and promised to do whatever God wanted—though healing was a medical impossibility. Ron prayed to God, "If you return the feeling in my hands and feet, then I will spend the rest of my life spoiling Betty Wiseman."

The Wednesday before Easter, Betty and Ron's mother came into the room with Ron's Bible and opened it on his chest. They began praying. Wiseman's two-year-old, Cindy, came in unnoticed. Cindy clutched Ron's big toe for five minutes and repeated the words, "Jesus, Jesus." Betty tapped Ron's cheek and pointed to Cindy. Ron recalled, "As I raised my head and looked at Cindy, the Lord healed me. I could feel her squeezing my toe." While feeling was instantly restored, muscle coordination took the next year for a full recovery because Ron had to relearn how to sit and walk.

The strife in your marriage may not be as desperate as Ron Wiseman's. It took drastic measures for Ron to change his life. Through communication with our Heavenly Father, you can see dramatic changes in your marriage.

Let's pray:

⊠

Prayer to Have Self-control

God, your word says that "he that has no rule over his own spirit is like a city that is broken down and without walls." With my relationships with my wife, I desperately need to exercise self-control and temperance.

Lord, I know that if faith, virtue, and knowledge dwell in me, I will bear much fruit. I repent of the times where I've been out of control. Strengthen me in my inner man by your Spirit so I can develop the fruit of self-control in my life.

Assist me to capture my thoughts and temper, then bring them into obedience of Christ. Thank you, Lord, for being the master of my life.

Amen.

⊠

Prayer for Unity in My Marriage

Gracious God, help me to have a spirit of oneness and unity with my wife. As her husband, help me to be a bridge-builder in our relationship. You say in the Bible that blessed are the peacemakers for they will see God. I long to have that sort of peace reign in my marriage and life.

You also command us as men to leave our parents and to cleave to our wife. Give me this longing of my heart for unity with my mate—in all the ways of my life— physically, emotionally, and spiritually. Bind us together, Lord, in a precious unity.

Father, it is through unity that you've said the people around us will know we are one. Reunite our relationship,

I pray. For it is pleasant in your sight when we dwell in unity. In every conversation and situation, give me the strength to work toward unity. Help me to be a man who forbears in love and help us to never have division in our home because we are united in you.

Manifest your abundant grace, love, harmony, and unity in our marriage relationship.

Amen.

⬦

Prayer to Live in Peace

Father God, as a man help me to live in peace with my wife. Guard my tongue from speaking evil toward my mate—whether she is in my presence or not.

Lord Jesus, you are the Prince of Peace, I will trust in you because you are the author and finisher of my faith. Don't allow me to make excuses for the strife and difficulties in my relationship with my wife. I don't want to live in denial or try to push hard situations out of my life. Instead remind me how a soft answer turns away wrath.

Keep me, I pray, as a man of perfect peace. I will seek to acknowledge you in all my ways. Thank you, God, for your peace which is ruling in my heart and life.

Amen.

⬦

Prayer for Gentleness and Kindness

God, you are gentle and kind. I want to be a man who lives with your interest and heart in this area of my life.

I freely admit that I live in a world which promotes violence and a sort of macho, "I'm in control" treatment for women. Instead, teach me to be a gentle man. Keep me from harshness and rudeness in my relationship with my wife. Help me, I pray, to live as a man that is meek in spirit. Adorn my inner self with a heart of kindness and gentleness which is incorruptible. I long to build such qualities in my life instead of financial or physical treasures which rust and rot. Thank you that these values such as kindness and gentleness will last forever.

Father, bring other men into my life who will exhibit these qualities. Teach me through these godly men and help me to follow their example as well as the example of heroes from the Bible. I commit my life into your hands and ask for you to fill me with a gentle spirit in my life.

Amen.

⊠

BIBLE VERSES ABOUT STRIFE WITH YOUR WIFE

As surely as a wind from the north brings rain, so a gossiping tongue causes anger! It is better to live alone in the corner of an attic than with a *contentious wife* in a lovely home. (Proverbs 25:23–24, NLT)

And you *husbands must love your wives* with the same love Christ showed the church. He gave up his life for her to make her holy and clean, washed by baptism and God's word. He did this to present her to himself as a glorious church without a spot or wrinkle or any other blemish. Instead, she will be holy and without fault. In the same way, husbands ought to love their wives as they love their own bodies. For a man is actually loving himself when he loves his wife.

No one hates his own body but lovingly cares for it, just as Christ cares for his body, which is the church. And we are his body. As the Scriptures say, "A man leaves his father and mother and is joined to his wife, and the two are united into one." This is a great mystery, but it is an illustration of the way Christ and the church are one.

So again I say, each man must love his wife as he loves himself, and the wife must respect her husband. (Ephesians 5:25–33, NLT)

Drink water from your own well—*share your love only with your wife.* Why spill the water of your springs in public, having sex with just anyone? You should reserve it for yourselves. Don't share it with strangers.

Let your wife be a fountain of blessing for you. Rejoice in the wife of your youth. She is a loving doe, a graceful deer. Let her breasts satisfy you always. May you always be captivated by her love. (Proverbs 5:15–18, NLT)

Live happily with the woman you love through all the meaningless days of life that God has given you in this world. The wife God gives you is your reward for all your earthly toil.

Whatever you do, do well. For when you go to the grave, there will be no work or planning or knowledge or wisdom. I have observed something else in this world of ours. The fastest runner doesn't always win the race, and the strongest warrior doesn't always win the battle. The wise are often poor, and the skillful are not necessarily wealthy. And those who are educated don't always lead successful lives. It is all decided by chance, by being at the right place at the right time.

People can never predict when hard times might come. Like fish in a net or birds in a snare, people are often caught by sudden tragedy. (Ecclesiastes 9:9–12, NLT)

CHAPTER 10

Prayers for Your Children

⊠

A Story About Children

The news was too overwhelming for Van Bruner at first. His only son, Scottie, was dying of sickle-cell anemia, and Van Bruner turned to alcohol. Then the mother of an old friend said, "Call a man of God."

Van looked at the woman like she was crazy and asked, "Are you some kind of fanatic? I need a scientific answer. . . . what do you mean, 'a man of God'? Come on!"

That night, Scottie collapsed in severe pain and was rushed to the hospital. The disease was attacking his spleen. The doctors shook their heads and said, "There is nothing we can do."

Suddenly Van felt cornered, without anyplace to turn, then he decided to call the "man of God." It turned out the man wasn't a minister but a janitor with a big smile. When the "man of God" reached their home, he talked with Van and his wife Lillian about a relationship with Christ. The trio prayed to have a personal relationship with Christ. Then he accompanied the parents to the hospital.

When they walked inside, the doctor was walking around in a daze. He looked up and said, "I don't know what happened. But Scottie's hemoglobin is way up. Above what it should be!"

"Praise God!" Van Bruner laughed. "God did that!" The healing in Scott Bruner was complete and today he's an assistant district attorney in Cook County, Illinois. In our fast-paced life, suddenly we wake up and our days with our children have disappeared. Especially as the children grow older and into teenagers, they seem to follow their peers instead of our guidance. These reasons drive us to pray for our children—no matter what their age—newborn or adult.

Let's pray:

◇

Prayer for Children to Have a Long-term Relationship with God

Father, thank you that you listen and hear my prayers. In our finite world, so often we don't exactly know what we're doing tomorrow much less a year from now. Yet you, God, stand outside the confines of time and space. In your wisdom, you can see the beginning from the end and you already know the plan for our lives.

We know from the Bible that you have plans for good and that we prosper. Lord, today, I want to pray for ————. ———— is your child even though I'm the earthly father. I pray that you would help me teach ———— about his heavenly Father. In your sovereignty, God, you made each of us with a free will and spirit to choose you or reject you. First, thank you that you gave us this spirit and didn't create robots. Yet because of it, each of us—

including my children—has a choice to make with his life. They can live for you or they can reject you.

I pray for you to place a protective hedge around ————. Guide him through my life and those around him into a long-term relationship with you. Help him to daily follow the paths of righteousness for your namesake.

Amen.

⊠

Prayer for Your Children's Friends and Social Skills

Heavenly Father, the Bible says that a friend sticks closer than a brother or a blood relative. My children need friends—people that they can trust; people who can share the good and bad times of life with them. I pray that you will lead and guide their lives to these quality friends. The friends may not be ones that I would choose, but give me an acceptance and grace for these friends.

God, show favor in the lives of my children. Please give them friends who know you and beyond a simple head knowledge—give them friends who love you. Help these friends to sharpen my children's relationship with you. A Proverb in the Bible says, "As iron sharpens iron, so one man sharpens another." I pray that the friends of my children will sharpen their lives and give them a deeper desire to know you—every minute of every day.

We can't live the lives of our children. So when it comes to this area of their friends, I release this area into your capable hands. As I pray, you can guide my children to these close friendships. Move in my life so I have the proper sense of balance for this area. I want to give my children the right opportunities for friendships yet not totally manipulate and control these friendships. I release my children and their social relationships into the hands of God.

Amen.

⊗

Prayer for "What Matters Most"

Father, I ask that you will help ——— by your power and love to set priorities. Permit ——— to earnestly seek first your kingdom from the wisdom that is found in the Bible. Help ——— to put his school, work assignment, and church activities in the right and proper perspective. Allow ——— to tell other people about you by placing you first in their priorities. Give him a sense that if he honors you first and then me as a parent, through keeping these priorities, he will experience a new level of happiness and peace.

Thank you, Father, for putting in my heart the desire to pray for ——— and helping in this crucial area.

Amen.

⊗

Prayer for Protection of Children

Heavenly Father, from my own life and from the Bible, I understand there is evil in the world. The battle between good and evil is constantly evident in my daily life.

As parents, we want to shield and protect our children from the forces of evil. I know that's not realistic because no matter what sort of protection I place around their lives, evil will still forge into the picture. So today, I'm asking you to undertake in an area beyond my capability. I need you to protect and guide my children from evil and harm's way. Please use me as a constant force of love and reassurance in my children's lives. But for those times when I am not around and evil springs into their lives, I pray for your guidance and protection.

Help my children to live every day in your care and to follow the truth in your words from the Bible.

Lord, I want to acknowledge that my children will at some point give in to temptation and sin. You tell us that "all have sinned and fall short of the glory of God." When my children move away from you and sin, I pray in the strong name of Jesus that they will turn to you for forgiveness. In advance, I want to thank you for the health and favor of that process of moving into a deeper relationship with you. You say, "If we confess our sins, he is faithful and just and will forgive us our sins and purify us from all unrighteousness." (1 John 1:9, NIV)

So, Lord, today I ask for your protective hand on my children.

Amen.

⊗

Prayer for Child Who has Drifted from God

Father God, I know that my son/daughter is not living in a manner which is pleasing to you! I pray that no evil or calamity will come on my children. I ask that you will guard them from accidents, physical sickness, or tragedy and protect them by the great power of your care and concern.

Heavenly Father, I know that you are a promise keeper. Keep my child by your promise you've declared that children are an inheritance from you and that angels are encamped around them. Allow my children to not live in fear but to be strong and courageous. Thank you, Lord, for giving them rest and peace. Thank you for protecting them.

Amen.

⊠

Prayer for Their Future Mates

Heavenly Father, we have many relationships with people through the course of our lives. Our children have many friends and acquaintances—in their school, in houses of worship, in our neighbors and other places. Yet one relationship stands out more than any others— their future husband or wife.

My child is only ——— years old. Whether he is young or a teenager, I want to ask for your direction and involvement in this particular relationship. As Wayne Watson wrote in his song, "Watercolour Ponies," "Seems an endless mound of laundry and a stairway laced with toys gives a blow-by-blow reminder of the war. That we fight for their well-being for their greater understanding to impart a holy reverence for the Lord."

Lord, guide my child to a mate that is your choice for his life. He needs a wife who will help him be a better person and support anything he attempts with encouragement and love. While, for now, I and my wife have had the most active involvement in his life, through adulthood I know his mate will deeply affect his life.

Our world is filled with divorce and people who make poor choices and poor decisions. You say in the Bible that "you hate divorce." That's a strong word but a strong feeling matches it. So I ask for your protection and guidance in his young life. Whether he ever acknowledges it or not, my child needs your hand of wisdom in his life. Thank you for your provision of a godly mate for my child.

Amen.

⊠

Prayer for Children to Pursue the Heart of God

Lord, we know that you are in control of the universe. As the Psalmist tells us, you control the rivers and you also control the heart of the king. While I'm concerned about the leadership of our nation, I'm coming to you about a personal matter in my family—my children.

Heavenly Father, you know ———. In fact, you knew them before they were born and while they were in their mother's womb. I want to ask that you would help ——— to be someone who knows you—not only knows you intellectually with his mind but someone who follows your will and desires with his heart and daily life.

I'm not pretending that to follow you will be easy. Temptations and wrong choices will present themselves to my children. When they have a wrong or bad choice for a possibility, please grant them your mind and wisdom to make a good choice. As only you can do through the power of your Spirit, draw my children into your arms and help them to follow you each day. Create a thirst in their heart for your words in the Bible. Give them the desire and longing to read the Bible and to memorize the words, then to use these words throughout the day—and especially when they face wrong choices. We can follow the example of your Son, Jesus, in the desert. When the devil tempted Jesus, he quoted from the Bible. Help my children to remember and use your words in their every-day life.

Guide them into integrity and honest living in a world which promotes deceit and deception. Use me in these efforts to guide them into a heart which loves you. Help me to be diligent about teaching them the Bible and taking them to church and other opportunities to learn about you. Begin in my own life today, then help that beginning to flow into my children so they love and honor you throughout this day.

Amen.

⊠

BIBLE VERSES ABOUT CHILDREN

When Samuel was old enough to eat, Hannah took him to the house of the Lord at Shiloh, along with a three-year-old bull, one half-bushel of flour, and a leather bag filled with wine. After they had killed the bull for the sacrifice, Hannah brought Samuel to Eli. She said to Eli, "As surely as you live, sir, I am the same woman who stood near you praying to the Lord. I prayed for this *child*, and the Lord answered my prayer and gave him to me. Now I give him back to the Lord. He will belong to the Lord all his life." And he worshiped the Lord there.

Hannah prayed: "The Lord has filled my heart with joy; I feel very strong in the Lord. I can laugh at my enemies; I am glad because you have helped me! There is no one holy like the Lord. There is no God but you; there is no Rock like our God. Don't continue bragging, don't speak proud words. The Lord is a God who knows everything, and he judges what people do.

"The bows of warriors break, but weak people become strong. Those who once had plenty of food now must work for food, but people who were hungry are hungry no more. The woman who could not have children now has seven, but the woman who had many children now is sad.

"The Lord sends death, and he brings to life. He sends people to the grave, and he raises them to life again. The Lord makes some people poor, and others he makes rich. He makes some people humble, and others he makes great. The Lord raises the poor up from the dust, and he lifts the needy from the ashes. He lets the poor sit with princes and receive a throne of honor.

"The foundations of the earth belong to the Lord, and the Lord set the world upon them. He protects those who are loyal to him, but evil people will be silenced in darkness. Power is not the key to success. The Lord destroys his enemies; he will thunder in heaven against them. The Lord will judge all the earth. He will give power to his king and make his appointed king strong." (1 Sam 1:24–1 Samuel 2:10, NCV)

And as we live in God, our love grows more perfect. So we will not be afraid on the day of judgment, but we can face him with confidence because we are like Christ here in this world. Such love has no fear because perfect love expels all fear. If we are afraid, it is for fear of judgment, and this shows that his love has not been perfected in us.

We love each other as a result of his loving us first. If someone says, "I love God," but hates another Christian, that person is a liar; for if we don't love people we can see, how can we love God, whom we have not seen? And God himself has commanded that we must love not only him but our Christian brothers and sisters, too.

Everyone who believes that Jesus is the Christ is a *child* of God. And everyone who loves the Father loves his *children*, too. We know we love God's children if we love God and obey his commandments. (1 John 4:17–1 John 5:2, NLT)

CHAPTER 11

Prayers for Parents or Other Loved Ones

◇

A Story About Parents

As a young boy, Chuck Colson often sat on the back porch with his father. Staring off into space, his father would tell Chuck about some of the great courtroom trials—for instance, the famous "Monkey" trial where two lawyers, Clarence Darrow and William Jennings Bryan, argued about the theory of evolution. As a young boy, Chuck developed his interest in law. Years later, Chuck worked ten feet from the President of the United States as his special counsel.

On those back steps, Chuck learned a life-changing lesson from his dad. Talking about excellence, Mr. Colson explained, "Whatever you put your mind to, you can do. Whatever you do in life—it doesn't matter if it's cleaning toilets—do it well. Do it with excellence. That's part of the dream of living in America. If you work hard, if you put your mind to it, you can succeed, you can get to the top."

Our parents guide our young lives and inspire us to achieve

beyond our own capacity. Whether you've had this type of parent or not, in our lives, each of us comes to a stark conclusion—we cannot change the parents that we have been given. Every parent makes mistakes—the only perfect parent is God, the Heavenly Father.

The Bible encourages us to pray for our parents and loved ones. We honor them with our prayers—whether they have a personal relationship with God or not. Our prayers for our parents is another part of interceding for others—yet it touches our emotions in a deep way because we are praying for a dear relative.

Let's pray:

◇

Prayer for My Parents' Needs

Lord, you alone know all of my parents' needs. I pray that you will open your hand of provision and satisfy their situation.

I thank you, God, that you say in the Bible how you have blessed them with every spiritual blessing in the heavenly places in Christ. I ask you God to supply all of my parents' needs according to your riches in glory and that my parents would lack for no good thing because they abide in you and your words abide in them. Father, I pray that you will prompt them by your Holy Spirit and that they will listen carefully to your guidance about how to spend their income so that their soul will delight in your abundant provision. Thank you, God, in advance for how you are meeting their every need.

Amen.

◇

Prayer for Loved Ones to Walk in Blessing

God, your Word says, "Blessed is the man unto whom God imputeth righteousness." Thank you for showing ——— that the way to walk in blessings during this life is through a consistent relationship with your Son Jesus Christ.

May ——— delight in your words in the Bible and grant ——— to taste and see that you are good and that you desire for them to be blessed wherever they are right now—whether in the city or in the country. Dear God, your blessings are greater than the details of this life. Grant ——— your spiritual favor and allow them to become rich in their daily knowledge of you so that they become spiritually prosperous.

Amen.

◇

Prayer for Peaceful Sleep

Gracious God, I know that sleep is a gift from you. Because we receive this gift from you, O Lord, you can make ——— lay down in peace and sleep. Thank you that deep, peaceful, and restful sleep comes from your hand.

It seems like in our hurried rushed world, each of us is loaded with many cares and burdens. Thank you that because ——— knows you, there is a place for us to unload these cares and burdens. You say in the Bible that we should come to you if we are feeling burdened because your burden is easy. I'm asking that ——— will be able to release these burdens into your capable hands then they can experience rest. I pray for ——— to have your help and a sweet sleep. I pray that when ——— is troubled or anxious, that he will remember that he can cast all of his cares on you because you care for him. Thank you that you make ——— to dwell in safety.

Amen.

⊠

Prayer for Parents in the Hospital or Nursing-home Care

Heavenly Father, I pray for my parent who is in the hospital or in nursing-home care. I pray that the light of your life would shine in the midst of any darkness. Lord, you are her shepherd and she shall not want for anything. I pray you will bring encouragement to her.

You are her strength and shield, and the glory and lifter of her head. Father, you have purposed for her and you do not desire it to be set aside. Help her to continue bringing forth fruit in her age for your Glory, God, and nothing is too hard for you. Show forth the Glory of your salvation on behalf of my parent who is in the hospital or in nursing-home care.

Amen.

⊠

BIBLE VERSES ABOUT PARENTS

The Lord said to Moses, "Tell all the people of Israel: 'I am the Lord your God. You must be holy because I am holy. You must respect *your mother and father*, and you must keep my Sabbaths. I am the Lord your God.'" (Leviticus 19:3, NCV)

. . .

Jesus answered, "And why do you refuse to obey God's command so that you can follow your own teachings? God said, 'Honor *your father and your mother*,' and 'Anyone who says cruel things to his father or mother must be put to death.'

"But you say a person can tell his father or mother, 'I have something I could use to help you, but I have given it to God already.' You teach that person not to honor his father or his mother. You rejected what God said for the sake of your own rules.

"You are hypocrites! Isaiah was right when he said about you: 'These people show honor to me with words, but their hearts are far from me. Their worship of me is worthless. The things they teach are nothing but human rules.' "

After Jesus called the crowd to him, he said, "Listen and understand what I am saying. It is not what people put into their mouths that makes them unclean. It is what comes out of their mouths that makes them unclean." (Matthew 15:3–11, NCV)

Listen to *your father*, who gave you life, and do not forget *your mother* when she is old. Learn the truth and never reject it. Get wisdom, self-control, and understanding.

The father of a good child is very happy; parents who have wise children are glad because of them. Make your father and mother happy; give your mother a reason to be glad. (Proverbs 23:22–25, NCV)

Children, obey *your parents* as the Lord wants, because this is the right thing to do. The command says, "Honor your father and mother." This is the first command that has a promise with it—"Then everything will be well with you, and you will have a long life on the earth." (Ephesians 6:1–3, NCV)

CHAPTER 12

Prayers for Your Neighbors

◇

A STORY ABOUT NEIGHBORS

Former Dallas Cowboy quarterback Roger Staubach learned some early lessons about neighbors. In *First Down, Lifetime to Go* he recounts overhearing his mother as a young man. A black family was moving into the neighborhood and people were in an uproar. Staubach's mother chastised the neighbors about their prejudice and Roger heard the conversation even though he was in another room of the home.

"How can you call yourself Christians?" his mother said. "How can you hold something over blacks because of the color of their skin, whether they want to move in next door or whatever they want to do? It goes against everything we believe as Christians."

This mother's conversation had a life-changing effect on her soon-to-be-famous son. He was taught to judge another person on who he is and what he stands for instead of his color. As Staubach writes, "Jesus Christ would jump out of His skin at such a two-faced attitude. The second greatest of the Ten Commandments is to love your neighbor as yourself. Yet there have been Christians through the years who've prevented people from joining their church because of skin color. This is a disgrace. There is no worse hypocrisy in all of life than a Christian prejudiced toward another human being."

You might not have a difficulty with your neighbor which relates to skin color. It could be a different relational problem or maybe you don't know your neighbor. In today's world, people live in almost total anonymity and isolation. Whether you are well acquainted with your neighbors or don't know their names, through prayer you can love them, bless them, and influence their lives.

Let's pray:

◇

Prayer for Friendship with Neighbors

Heavenly Father, your Word says that a man that has friends must show himself friendly. Also the Bible says, there is a friend that will stick closer than a brother. Lord Jesus, help me to understand the importance of friendship. I want to exhibit the care and support that a friend should show to others. Help me, God, to become the kind of friend that will be a brother even in times of adversity.

Amen.

◇

Prayer for Salvation of Neighbors

Precious Lord, I want to thank you for the gift of salvation through your Son Jesus Christ. I pray that you will work in ———'s life so that he/she will call on you and be saved. Please send your laborers into ———'s life to share the Good News about Jesus Christ. May ———'s eyes be open to the truth of your Word. Thank you, Lord, for calling ——— to yourself and for using me to pray for his/her eternal salvation.

Amen.

⌖

Prayer for a Neighbor's Healing

Thank you, God, for your healing power and that you desire to heal individuals who ask for your healing touch. I pray for ——— who is suffering from ———, that you would heal his/her body and restore total health. You are the creator of our bodies and you are the one who brings healing to the body. In the Bible, you say, with your stripes we are healed (Isaiah 53). I thank you, God, that you are the same today as you were yesterday (Hebrews 13:8).

You have commanded us to pray for others that they may be healed and through my prayer of faith you would save the sick and raise them up. In faith, I pray for ——— and I ask you, God, to heal them as you healed the afflicted when you walked the earth. Thank you for healing ——— and bringing all glory to your name.

Amen.

⌖

Prayer for a Neighbor's Finances

Lord God, I pray to you for ——— who is having financial difficulty. God, I know that you desire for your people to prosper. I pray that his/her ways would be prosperous and that if there is anything that is preventing him/her from receiving your blessing, then you would reveal your word and insight to ———. Be with ——— in this time of need. Riches are a gift from you and I pray that you would grant your blessings to ———. I believe, therefore, that all of ———'s needs will be met and you will make all grace, favor, and earthly blessings come to ——— in abundance.

Amen.

⬦

Prayer for a Neighbor Who Has Lost a Loved One

God, I pray for ——— who has lost his/her ———. I know that your Holy Spirit is the comforter and I pray that you would give him/her comfort at this time of sorrow and allow him/her in this time of mourning to be turned into your Joy. As ——— realizes that you have provided for his/her loved one, God, convert his/her sadness into joy. Help me pray ——— to see your power and to rejoice in anticipation of being reunited with their loved one.

Amen.

⬦

Prayer for a Neighbor's Troubled Marriage

Almighty God, I pray for the marriage of ———. I pray and confess that ——— will let all bitterness, wrath, resentment, clamor, slander, abuse, evil speaking, malice, and ill will be put away from them. Lord, I ask that ——— would arrive at an understanding of your will for their marriage and that they will love one another with the type of love that only God can give. I pray that ———— would be united in peace and harmony.

Today I stand in the gap for ———— and ask for your touch on their marriage relationship.

Amen.

◇

BIBLE VERSES ABOUT NEIGHBORS

One of the teachers of the law came and heard Jesus arguing with the Sadducees. Seeing that Jesus gave good answers to their questions, he asked Jesus, "Which of the commands is most important?"

Jesus answered, "The most important command is this: 'Listen, people of Israel! The Lord our God is the only Lord. Love the Lord your God with all your heart, all your soul, all your mind, and all your strength.'

"The second command is this: '*Love your neighbor as you love yourself.*' There are no commands more important than these."

The man answered, "That was a good answer, Teacher. You were right when you said God is the only Lord and there is no other God besides him. One must love God with all his heart, all his mind, and all his strength. And one must love his *neighbor* as he loves himself. These commands are more important than all the animals and sacrifices we offer to God."

When Jesus saw that the man answered him wisely, Jesus said to him, "You are close to the kingdom of God." And after that, no one was brave enough to ask Jesus any more questions. (Mark 12:28–34, NCV)

• • •

But the man, wanting to show the importance of his question, said to Jesus, "And who is my *neighbor?*"

Jesus answered, "As a man was going down from Jerusalem to Jericho, some robbers attacked him. They tore off his clothes, beat him, and left him lying there, almost dead. It happened that a Jewish priest was going down that road. When he saw the man, he walked by on the other side. Next, a Levite came there, and after he went over and looked at the man, he walked by on the other side of the road.

Then a Samaritan traveling down the road came to where the hurt man was. When he saw the man, he felt very sorry for him. The Samaritan went to him, poured olive oil and wine on his wounds, and bandaged them. Then he put the hurt man on his own donkey and took him to an inn where he cared for him.

The next day, the Samaritan brought out two coins, gave them to the innkeeper, and said, 'Take care of this man. If you spend more money on him, I will pay it back to you when I come again.' "

Then Jesus said, "*Which one of these three men do you think was a neighbor to the man who was attacked by the robbers?*"

The expert on the law answered, "The one who showed him mercy." Jesus said to him, "Then go and do what he did." (Luke 10:29–37, NCV)

Don't repay evil for evil. Don't snap back at those who say unkind things about you. Instead, pray for God's help for them, for we are to be kind to others, and God will bless us for it. If you want a happy, good life, keep control of your tongue, and guard your lips from telling lies.

Turn away from evil and do good. *Try to live in peace* even if you must run after it to catch and hold it! For the

Lord is watching his children, listening to their prayers; but the Lord's face is hard against those who do evil. Usually no one will hurt you for wanting to do good. But even if they should, you are to be envied, for God will reward you for it. (1 Peter 3:9–14, TLB)

CHAPTER 13

Prayers for Anger

◇

A STORY ABOUT ANGER

As men, we know the strength of anger. It can be used for productivity or destruction. The productive results of anger come from a challenge like, "You'll never be able to . . ." And you swell up and say (out loud or inside), "Oh yeah! I'll show you!" Then in anger, you throw yourself into the matter and it is resolved in a fraction of the expected time.

Or anger can be used in a destructive manner. Maybe your expression of anger erupts on the freeway when cut off from another driver. Or maybe your anger flows in a slow-building explosion which unexpectedly hits those around you—to their confusion. Or instead of erupting, your method for anger is stoic silence. One of my friends, Michael (not his real name), has always had a "short fuse." Sarah, his wife, continually fears his unleashed hostility. One day I talked with Sarah about a family issue which needed his input and Sarah decided not to risk an angry reaction. Later, I learned Michael's reactions were rooted in many childhood hurts. Instead of dealing with those hurts, Michael transformed his hurt into anger and resentment. In the long run, his reaction robbed him of intimacy with anyone and blocked his enjoyment of life.

Recently Michael went into the doctor for his annual physical exam. Walking into the room with his chart, the doctor said, "There's no reason you can't live a completely normal life as long as you try to enjoy it." Anger can prevent us from enjoying life.

When the emotion of anger bursts into your day, how do you handle it? The pundits encourage us to count to ten (or maybe a hundred) before any reaction. The counting doesn't change our circumstances but allows us a space of time for a proper perspective. If you take time to pray when you feel anger, it can provide much-needed perspective on the situation and help you not to unleash angry feelings.

Over ten years ago, I was the compliance officer at a Texas prison. I met men who acted out their anger in destructive and violent ways and now live behind bars. For their uncontrolled temper, they paid a high price and are now held in bondage. Your anger doesn't have to take you to prison, but it can certainly smash some lives and relationships around you. Through a connection to God and prayer, you can be freed from the emotional bondage of anger. For your first step, acknowledge the force of anger in your life. The following prayers will help you. I've personally prayed with hundreds of men who have sought help to be free from their anger.

Let's pray!

◇

Prayer as an Antidote to Anger

Father, in the Bible you say that we should be angry but not sin. (Ephesians 4:26) I want to tell you that it's hard to experience anger and also control the feelings and actions from anger. When these feelings rage through me, it's hard to control. I don't want to be known as an angry father or angry person. I'm asking for your divine help in my life. Help me to overcome and conquer my past actions from anger.

In the past, I've hurt people with my anger. Please forgive me for this hurt and give me your Wisdom and insight how to restore these relationships and build for the future. Give me the right words to say to these people and the perfect attitude for my response. When I ask these people for forgiveness and they lash back at me, help me to have love and compassion. Then I will have compassion as my answer instead of another round of anger and resentment.

God, I give you my life and my emotion of anger. Through your great power, I seek the evidence of your action in my life. Help me to develop love, joy, and peace in my heart, then to show these emotions to others in my path.

Amen.

⊗

Prayer to Turn from Anger to Apology

Father, I need to be brutally honest with you. Because of my pride, it's hard for me to apologize to anyone for anything. I don't want others to think that I'm weak and can't "be a man." (Whatever that really means!)

In fact, I've always found it difficult to say the words "I'm sorry." Yet at the same time, deep inside, I am sincerely sorry for my actions. Many times I've reacted in anger with my family, friends, relatives, and others who cross my path.

Show me how to seek forgiveness from other people and how to start my relationship fresh with these people. Help me to be slow to anger and to be in control of my emotions.

You, Lord, want me to have truth inside myself and outside with mankind. Give me the wisdom that I need to find truth and avoid anger. As the Psalmist prayed, "Create in me a clean heart, O God, and renew a right spirit within me."

Amen.

⊠

Prayer for Freedom from Anger

Lord, in the Bible, your Son said, "Whoever the son sets free is free indeed." (John 8:36) Instead I'm living in complete opposite of this spiritual truth. I am held captive because of my anger, and my strong feelings for people and circumstances has grown so large to become a stumbling block in my life. Help me to turn to you and trust you with all of my heart and not to lean on my own understanding. As I acknowledge you in all my ways, you promise to direct my path.

Free me from the power of wrath and give me the strength to stop my anger. You say those people who are hasty in spirit and angry appear as fools. I don't want to be foolish in your eyes or the eyes of my fellow man.

Lord God, you are my salvation and my joy. I pray that I can live in your liberty and freedom. Release me from the bondage of anger. I surrender my mind, will, and emotions into your capable hands. Provide me with grace to take control of this strong emotion. I am trusting you so I can experience a new level of liberty.

Amen.

◇

Prayer to Turn from Anger
to Blessing

Lord, you are the great God of change and transformation. You control the details of the weather as well as the details of our lives—provided we release control into your capable hands. I want you to change me from a person who is angry to a person with a place of honor and a blessing. At the moment, I am not living in your protective blessing and instead I've permitted my anger to ruin my life.

In the Bible, you promise to bless me with all of the spiritual blessings in Christ Jesus. I can't receive those blessings because anger erupts in my life. Father, I submit this strong emotion to Jesus Christ and to you, God. Take *total* control of my behavior—beginning with this moment. In faith and belief in your words which are in the Bible, I confess that I am moving from anger to blessing and to the abundance of your greatness!

Lord, I desire to prosper and to be in good physical health even as my soul prospers. I affirm that I will diligently obey your message in Scripture. Then, as the Psalmist describes, I can become like a tree firmly planted by streams of water which bear the fruit of your blessings in my life. (Psalm 1:3)

Amen.

⊠

Prayer to Turn from Anger to Forgiveness

Father, I make a fresh commitment to stop the destructive anger in my life and to live in peace and harmony with my family, friends, associates, and neighbors. Thank you, God, that you created mankind with a free will to make such decisions. I pray today will mark a milestone in my life and a total turning from anger and instead a turning toward peace.

I confess my inability to make this transformation on my own strength but I need your help through every minute and every hour. Also today I'm releasing all bitterness, resentment, strife, and unkindness from my past and even my forgotten past. I ask you to help me to forgive every person who has hurt or wronged me. I bring those people to you, name by name, then ask you to also cover those people who I can't remember. My desire, Father, is to live each day in peace and love. Help me to display mercy and forgiveness of others in my own life. I pray through the powerful name of your Son, that your forgiveness will flow into the lives of everyone I know to bring you honor.

Amen.

⊠

BIBLE VERSES ABOUT ANGER

You must display a new nature because you are a new person, created in God's likeness—righteous, holy, and true. So put away all falsehood and "tell your neighbor the truth" because we belong to each other.

And "don't sin by letting *anger* gain control over you."

Don't let the sun go down while you are still angry, for anger gives a mighty foothold to the Devil. (Ephesians 4:24–27, NLT)

So put to death the sinful, earthly things lurking within you. Have nothing to do with sexual sin, impurity, lust, and shameful desires. Don't be greedy for the good things of this life, for that is idolatry.

God's terrible *anger* will come upon those who do such things. You used to do them when your life was still part of this world. But now is the time to get rid of *anger*, rage, malicious behavior, slander, and dirty language. (Colossians 3:5–8, NLT)

Dear friends, be quick to listen, slow to speak, and slow to get *angry*. Your anger can never make things right in God's sight. So get rid of all the filth and evil in your lives, and humbly accept the message God has planted in your hearts, for it is strong enough to save your souls.

And remember, it is a message to obey, not just to listen to. If you don't obey, you are only fooling yourself. For if you just listen and don't obey, it is like looking at your face in a mirror but doing nothing to improve your appearance. (James 1:19–23, NLT)

CHAPTER 14

Prayers for Courage

◇

A STORY ABOUT COURAGE

The call for courage appears at odd times in our lives. Maybe you are faced with an unpopular decision in your family. Several of your family members are supportive but others contend you are making a major mistake, yet you know the decision is right. Do you have the internal strength to move ahead with your life or follow the mixed guidance from others?

Or your supervisor has walked into your office. "Here you go!" he says as he slaps the newest project on your desk. "It's ready-made for you." You wonder what in the world he's talking about and after he leaves, you discover that it's your first million-dollar project where you are in charge. Do you have the self-confidence to move ahead with courage? In multiple situations throughout our lives, we need courage to handle a particular situation.

One of my most challenging circumstances for courage came in 1986. My wife, Denise, was expecting our twin boys, Gabriel and Christian. At twenty-six weeks into the pregnancy, she developed severe complications. With Denise in the hospital, her physician took me aside and said, "Steve, this condition is severe and in fact, Denise and the twins have a slim chance for survival."

The news hit me like someone picked up a two-by-four and smashed me. Talk about a wake-up call! I felt totally weak and knew that I needed courage from God to pull me through this family crisis. Initially, I complained to God, saying, "Lord, this is not supposed to happen. My wife has three more months in this pregnancy." Immediately I was confronted with some major decisions which affected each member of my family. My only hope was to find courage from God through prayer.

I turned to the Bible for some examples of courage in desperate times. One of the greatest leaders for the Jewish people was Moses. When Moses received the Ten Commandments, another person was on the mountain—Joshua. Throughout the leadership of Moses, Joshua was his assistant and understudy. One day God told Moses that he was going to die. Suddenly Joshua was faced with the daunting task of leading the Jewish people into the Promised Land. In such a demanding situation, Joshua needed courage to continue. I'm sure he felt alone as the leader—just like I felt alone in that hospital. Just like Joshua, I focused on God for courage. In Joshua chapter 1, God commanded Joshua "to be strong and of good courage."

Great advice, yet how is it executed? From my experience, it is through prayer with God, and intimate solitude. In prayer, God molds champions and gives them the courage to face the challenges of life.

While my wife was unconscious in the delivery room, initially I looked around at family and friends. I hoped to find my courage in these caring people. Many of them were sincere in their concern yet none of them could give me the dose of courage that I desperately needed. In prayer, I began to draw on the bank of experiences with God in my life. As a man, I had learned to pursue God for each step and each decision. From my small steps in the past, God prepared me to have courage. It's not a one-time deposit into a bank account but a daily turning to God for courage with various decisions. Daniel was an old man in the Bible when he was thrown into the den of lions. For years, he had cultivated a relationship with God. He drew on that relationship for courage and God's ability to protect him from the lions. Or look at Noah building the huge boat known as an ark. It was on completely dry land and took many years of hard work. The crowd around Noah taunted him at his efforts saying, "Hey, Noah. Why are you building a boat on dry land?" The only answer was that God told Noah to build the boat. It took great courage for Noah to continue in such a decision.

From the doctors, I knew my wife's situation was critical. She was only given a 30 percent chance to survive. Our two unborn sons weighed a little over a pound each and the doctors gave them even slimmer odds for survival. My only option seemed to ask God for courage. Typical for such an occasion, many friends and family were eager to visit my wife and give their advice. While my wife was in the hospital, I had to summon my courage to restrict even our most intimate friends and family from frequent visitation. Many of them didn't understand my protection and insistence. In the face of those difficult decisions, I took my courage from God. In time, my decision proved the best for Denise's welfare, but it wasn't an easy course of action.

I took my courage and strength from God, and after a three-month hospital stay, my wife came home, and a few days later, the healthy twins followed. Drawing on courage from God, there were several immediate results. First, my family pulled through the crisis and came home. A more lasting result from my courage was a healthy respect for God's power in my life. Through prayer, I learned that courage pulled me through a sudden trauma.

Let's pray:

◇

Prayer for Courage in Weakness

Lord, as a man, I hate to admit something to you. Yes, you know it already since you are the Creator of heaven and earth. You see the entire picture of our lives before they are even lived out—our joys, our successes, and our failures. At this particular moment in time, I hate to admit it but I'm feeling weak. I'm full of uncertainty about the future of ———— situation. I can't see how this situation will end and it's looking pretty desperate. I need a dose of courage for my weakness. Infuse my life and heart with the strength to move ahead and follow your directions.

Father, teach me to model my life after the men in the Bible. Many of them were weak—like when David attacked the giant Goliath. He looked pretty weak out there against that huge armored giant. David carried a simple sling and five smooth stones. Lord, help me to have courage to attack the weaknesses of my life—just like David attacked the giant. The small shepherd boy was victorious and I want to have your victory in my life over this weakness.

It is hard to admit a weakness to you, God. I know you have the power and love for victory over this situation. Thank you for the provision of such courage to overcome weakness.

Amen.

⌖

Prayer for Courage for Self-confidence

Father, at this moment, I'm not feeling confident. You know and understand this situation as only God can understand it. Your Scriptures say that you are my strength and my shield. Help me to grasp the reality of this promise in my life today. Through your heavenly power, you can infuse my life with the courage for self-confidence and give me strength.

Sure, some people may laugh or taunt me or say that was a foolish move. In the face of such feelings, I can rely on you, Lord. I turn to you and ask for you to be my shield. Wrap your heavenly arms around me and protect me from the fiery darts of discouragement or doubt and instead give me the self-confidence that I need for today.

Because the Bible says faith is the assurance of things hoped for and the conviction of things not seen (Hebrews 11:1), I'm reaching out in faith and asking for self-confidence and courage. I thank you, Lord, that you are working in my heart and life. Through this working you continue to give me courage and help me grow in your grace and love.

Amen.

⌖

Prayer for Courage to Love

Father, I'm going to be completely honest with you today. It's difficult for me to love others. There are a litany of things that I can blame it on: we live in a "me"-centered world where everything evolves around "my" wants and needs. Or I can blame it on my upbringing and family relationships. Or I can even face my own fears and say I'm simply afraid to love others. I need talk with you honestly—man-to-man—and let you know I accept responsibility for my lack of love. I need to have love for others.

Lord, the Bible declares that we can have love for others because you first loved us. Thank you for reaching out to mankind and me in particular with your loving touch of grace. You have declared that of the greatest virtues—faith, hope, and love—the greatest is love. Help me to accept how you have reached out to me in love, then in turn let me have love for others. I open my heart and life to accept the powerful force of your love in my life.

Father, teach me or show me how to love the people that cross my path today. Whether they are family members, neighbors, coworkers, or someone in the grocery store, help me to show love. Please forgive me for my failures in the past. I've taken the easy way out and not loved the people around me. Sometimes when I've seen people in need, I've turned away and thought, "Let someone else take care of that situation." Thank you that you offer me forgiveness for my failure to love or to even have the courage to love.

Lord, increase my capacity to love the people that I will contact today. When people notice a difference in my life, help me to give you the credit for your help. As wounded, needy, or broken-hearted people cross my path, give me the words or the practical experience to be an encouragement in their life. Thank you for the powerful force of love and give me the courage to use this powerful force in my relationships.

Amen.

⊠

Prayer for Courage in Decisions

Lord, I need your courage for some tough decisions that are right in front of me. There are a myriad of possibilities in my decisions. A wrong step may lead me down a path toward destruction in a domino type of effect.

First, Lord, I want to thank you for flexibility. As I understand your Scriptures, you are not some ogre that is sitting around waiting for me to make a wrong decision then will say, "Gotcha." Instead there is a sphere of decisions where you have given me free will to select and choose. In other words, you can equally bless and move in several different directions. I'm asking that you will give me the courage to make a wise decision and that you will guide my decision.

Then, Lord, I need your touch so that I can be free to start over today with this decision. Then, in that freedom, I can avoid such pitfalls as procrastination and indecisiveness. If I'm honest, I'll admit I have fallen into such pitfalls in the past. I've wasted time and energy in worry and fear and simple indecision. With your involvement, I want to avoid such a trap today.

In a series of small decisions and occasionally some major ones, I walk down the path of life. I'm asking, God, for your assistance in the decisions—large and small. Infuse my life with courage for these decisions. Help me to rest and be assured of your best interest for my future. Thank you for being such a loving God. You aren't too big or too busy for any decision, large or small. Through your availability and assistance give me the courage for today's decisions.

Amen.

◇

Prayer for Courage in Home and Relationships

Father, forgive me for passing the buck in my home and relationships. I admit that I have not followed your directions to be the man that you want me to be or to provide the spiritual leadership for my home.

I want to be a better man, husband, father, leader, and a godly man. With your touch and help, free me from not taking any action and the sin of passivity. Help me to take the initiative in my home. I need your courage and strength in this important area of my life.

Give me a greater appreciation for the relationships you have given me with my family, friends, and coworkers. In the past, I've tried sometimes to act on my own and without your guidance. Help me not to attempt to succeed without you.

Today bring other men into my life who can help me grow in this area. As Proverbs says, "As iron sharpens iron, so one man sharpens another." Give me the relationships with other men who can sharpen my life and help me have courage in relationships.

Amen.

◇

Prayer for Calmness in the Midst of Difficulties

Father, an emotion has been unleashed in my mind and heart. I'm loaded with fear and it drives my thoughts and actions. It disturbs people around me because fear makes me feel out of control. I'm asking in your mighty power to fill my life today with a new emotion and source of comfort. I need your peace and calmness to fill the well of my emotions. Take control of my life and heart.

Years ago, one of the greatest kings was on the earth, named David. He left us with many Psalms about fear and how you can take control of our fears. Like you helped David in the ancient days, help me, Lord, with my fears. As David said, "When I am afraid, I will trust in you."

Lord, it's a bit unusual, but I want to thank you for bringing this difficulty and fearful situation into my life and heart. Instead of allowing fear to consume my life, I want to ask that we use this circumstance as an opportunity to build even greater trust in you and how you work in my life and heart. Instead of fear and doubts, I pray you would sweep my heart clean with your peace and control.

Peace is a virtue which comes from you. As Jesus Christ said, "My peace I leave with you. Not as the world gives but I give you." Help us to rest in the knowledge that you will control in a way that we cannot. We surrender our fears into your capable hands.

Amen.

◇

Prayer for Trust in Times of Uncertainty

God, your name is on every single coin in our pocket and every bill in our wallet. These coins and bills include the words, "In God We Trust." Our founding fathers knew that they should continually place their trust in you. Uncertainty filled their lives yet they knew that their faith and trust should be in your guidance.

Today, my life comes face-to-face with an uncertain situation. You know the details of this situation and you even know how it will end before it ends. Thank you that you are the God who cares about his people and guides our lives and every move and thought. Help me to focus on you in the midst of the uncertainty. I ask for you to give me the faith and trust for this situation. When Jesus was on the earth, a man asked Jesus to heal his epileptic son and used the phrase "if you can." Jesus instantly replied, "If you can? All things are possible for God." The man realized he had offended Jesus and said, "Sir, I believe, help my unbelief."

Today we ask for you, Heavenly Father, to help our unbelief. Strengthen us for the day and the uncertainty. We give this uncertain situation into your capable hands. We thank you and rest in your love and guidance.

Amen.

⊠

Prayer for Bravery

Lord, sometimes the winds of life blow around me like a hurricane. If I'm honest, it frightens me. I want to stand before you as an honest man. Yes, I am afraid of the situation in front of me. It is full of uncertainty and full of possible things which could backfire.

In the middle of these fears, help me to seek you and your desire for this particular situation. I can't do it on my own strength. From past experience, I know that if I rely on my own energy and strength then I will fall flat on my face. I need your wisdom and calmness in the middle of the uncertainty and fears.

Heavenly Father, when I think of brave people, I instantly think of David fighting the giant Goliath with only five smooth stones. Or the strong man, Samson, fighting the Philistine army with the jawbone of a donkey. He killed so many men, Lord, with such a simple weapon! I can't imagine how Samson and David stood their ground for those situations. Fear must have been present but you gave them a measure of bravery and courage to stand their ground.

Today, I'm facing a different battle. It may be in my home or family, or more emotional than physical. I need your inspiration and bravery for this situation. I ask in your strong name to take away my fears and fill the vacuum with your Heavenly wisdom and bravery.

Amen.

⊠

BIBLE VERSES ABOUT COURAGE

As the time of King David's death approached, he gave this charge to his son Solomon: "I am going where everyone on earth must someday go. Take *courage* and be a man. Observe the requirements of the Lord your God and follow all his ways. Keep each of the laws, commands, regulations, and stipulations written in the law of Moses so that you will be successful in all you do and wherever you go." (1 Kings 2: 1–3, NLT)

When people take an oath, they call on someone greater than themselves to hold them to it. And without any question that oath is binding. God also bound himself with an oath, so that those who received the promise could be perfectly sure that he would never change his mind.

So God has given us both his promise and his oath. These two things are unchangeable because it is impossible for God to lie. Therefore, we who have fled to him for refuge can take new *courage*, for we can hold on to his promise with confidence. This confidence is like a strong and trustworthy anchor for our souls. It leads us through the curtain of heaven into God's inner sanctuary. (Hebrews 6:16–19, NLT)

You, too, must be patient. And take *courage*, for the coming of the Lord is near. Don't grumble about each other, my brothers and sisters, or God will judge you. For look! The great Judge is coming. He is standing at the door!

For examples of patience in suffering, look at the prophets who spoke in the name of the Lord. We give great honor to those who endure under suffering. Job is an example of a man who endured patiently. From his experience we see how the Lord's plan finally ended in good, for he is full of tenderness and mercy. (James 5:8–11, NLT)

CHAPTER 15

Prayers for Sickness

◇

A Story About Sickness

Several years ago, a telephone call interrupted Chuck Swindoll's Friday afternoon. As he describes in *Flying Closer to the Flame*, Chuck learned his daughter Charissa had been in an accident at school. While practicing a human pyramid with her cheerleading squad, someone on the bottom slipped and the entire structure collapsed. Charissa was on the top and hit the back of her head with a sharp jolt. The blow made her legs and arms numb so she could not even move her fingers. After the school official called the paramedics, they notified Chuck.

At the time, Chuck's wife, Cynthia was away so he raced to the school to see his daughter. On the way, he prayed aloud to God and called out like a little child trapped in an empty well. Chuck asked for several things—to touch his daughter, for strength and skill and wisdom for the paramedics. Because he felt his tears near the surface, he asked God to calm him and to restrain the growing sense of panic. In the car, Chuck sensed God's presence in a fresh way. His pulse calmed down and as he arrived at the school parking lot, even the red-and-blue flashing emergency lights didn't seem to faze his calmness.

When Chuck arrived at the crowd, the paramedics had Charissa strapped to a stretcher and her neck was in a brace. Kneeling down beside her, Chuck kissed her forehead and heard her say, "I can't feel anything below my shoulders. Something snapped just below my neck." She was blinking through tears.

Under normal circumstances, Chuck would have been borderline out-of-control. He would have been shouting at the crowd or barking at the ambulance driver—but he didn't. Instead, Chuck calmly stroked her hair and whispered, "I'm here with you, sweetheart. So is our Lord. No matter what happens, we'll make it through this together. I love you, Charissa." Tears ran down the side of her face as she closed her eyes.

With patience and poise, Chuck dealt with the medical attendants and they agreed on which hospital and the route to get there. As Chuck followed in his car, he sensed again the Lord's profound guidance and presence. At the hospital, Chuck was joined by his wife Cynthia. Together the couple waited for the doctor's report and once more they prayed.

A few hours later, they learned that a vertebrae in Charissa's back had been fractured. Both the doctors wore grim faces and told the Swindolls they didn't know how long the numbness would last, or if it would. There was nothing medical for them to lean on so instead they cast themselves into the hands of a capable God.

Exhausted from the ordeal, Chuck still had to go to work as a pastor and preached three sermons Sunday morning. In human weakness and dependence on God, he spoke. His audio department has told him that the message is one of his most-requested tapes since he became a pastor in 1971.

And Charissa was wonderfully healed. Today she's a wife and mother who recalls the incident only when she sneezes—then her upper back hurts. If Chuck hears his daughter sneeze, it reminds him of a precious experience with God through prayer.

Let's pray:

⊠

Prayer for Physical Illness

Father God, I pray in faith that you will heal me from this sickness. Raise me up, I pray, O Lord. You have sent your truth from the Bible to deliver me from destruction. Jesus was wounded for my transgressions and bruised for my sins and by his stripes I am healed. The Bible also tells us, "Save me and I will be saved, heal me and I will be healed." I claim the reality of those words in my own situation.

The Bible also declares, "Healing is the children's bread, I am your child, Lord, and you are my refuge, my very present help in times of trouble, a strong tower that I can run inside and be safe. Thank you for sustaining me in my sickness. Grant me to live and not die that I may declare your great works. For great and mighty are you, O God, and greatly to be praised. May others see your works and proclaim your goodness.

Amen.

⊠

Prayer for Depression

Heavenly Father, I have come to the end of everything. I am struggling to break through sadness. Help me, I pray, to be motivated to try again. I ask you, dear Lord, to remove any depression that comes into my life. Your word declares that when I cry out to you, you will hear me and deliver me out of all my troubles. Help me to always pray and not lose heart, for you, O God, are my strength.

Grant me comfort from my tribulations, that I may be able to comfort those who are in trouble. I thank you that you are my God and I will trust in you. While my weeping may last for a night, I am assured through your Word that joy comes in the morning. You, dear God, are the lifter of my head.

Amen.

⬦

Prayer for Times of Weakness

Father God, I am so weak. I confess that at times I find it difficult to get out of bed. You have promised the comfort of the Holy Spirit to me during these times. Grant me the sense of your presence. Father, I know that when I am weak then you can make me strong.

I thank you, God, that as I pray, you will consider my affliction and deliver me, for I do not forget your law. I pray that you will plead my cause and redeem me. Because the Bible tells us that those who dwell in the secret place of the Most High will not be afraid of the terror by day or by night.

Thank you, Lord, for reviving me and strengthening me, according to your word. We know from the Bible that they who wait on you will renew their strength, they will mount up with wings of eagles, they will run and not be weary, walk and not faint. Thank you for granting me the strength to overcome.

Amen.

◈

Prayer for a Broken Heart

Almighty God, you know the hurt of my life. I pray that you would console me through your word. Wipe away my tears and bring joy to my life. Give me beauty for ashes and exchange the oil of joy for mourning, the garment of praise for the spirit of heaviness. Then others will call me a tree of righteousness.

Thank you, God, that your word is my comfort in times of affliction. Your word gives me life. Help me to live every day by faith and not by sight because my hope is rooted firmly in you.

Help me to cast all of my concerns on your broad shoulders because you care for me. I am confident that you will never leave me nor forsake me even until the end of my life. Thank you for granting me your joy and gladness. Touch my heart and bring healing to my soul, for you are the God of my salvation.

Amen.

◈

BIBLE VERSES ABOUT SICKNESS

Paul gathered a pile of brushwood and, as he put it on the fire, a viper, driven out by the heat, fastened itself on his hand. When the islanders saw the snake hanging from his hand, they said to each other, "This man must be a murderer; for though he escaped from the sea, Justice has not allowed him to live."

But Paul shook the snake off into the fire and suffered no ill effects. The people expected him to swell up or suddenly fall dead, but after waiting a long time and seeing nothing unusual happen to him, they changed their minds and said he was a god.

There was an estate nearby that belonged to Publius, the chief official of the island. He welcomed us to his home and for three days entertained us hospitably. His father was *sick* in bed, suffering from fever and dysentery. Paul went in to see him and, after prayer, placed his hands on him and healed him. When this had happened, the rest of the sick on the island came and were cured.

They honored us in many ways and when we were ready to sail, they furnished us with the supplies we needed. (Acts 28:3–10, NIV)

Is any one of you in trouble? He should pray. Is anyone happy? Let him sing songs of praise. Is any one of you *sick*? He should call the elders of the church to pray over him and anoint him with oil in the name of the Lord.

And the prayer offered in faith will make the sick person well; the Lord will raise him up. If he has sinned, he will be forgiven.

Therefore confess your sins to each other and pray for each other so that you may be healed. The prayer of a righteous man is powerful and effective. Elijah was a man just like us. He prayed earnestly that it would not rain, and it did not rain on the land for three and a half years. Again he prayed, and the heavens gave rain, and the earth produced its crops. (James 5:13–18, NIV)

CHAPTER 16

Prayers of Rejoicing

⊠

A STORY ABOUT REJOICING IN PRAYER

Shortly after the Dallas Theological Seminary was founded in 1924, it almost came to the point of bankruptcy. On that particular day, all of the creditors planned to foreclose on the school. On the morning of the foreclosure, in president Dr. Lewis Chafer's office, a number of the men from the seminary met for prayer. They were praying for a miracle of God's provision. Harry Ironside was one of the men in the meeting and he prayed, "Lord, we rejoice in you knowing that the cattle on a thousand hills are Thine. Please sell some of them and send us the money."

During the prayer meeting, a tall Texan who had boots and an open-collar shirt stepped into the business office. He said, "I just sold two carloads of cattle and feel compelled to give the money to the seminary. I don't know if they need it or not, but here's the check!"

The secretary took the check, and knowing the critical financial state of the school, went to the door of the prayer meeting and timidly knocked. When she finally got a response, Dr. Chafer took the check from her hand. It was exactly the amount of the debt! The president recognized the name on the check as a cattleman from Fort Worth. Turning to Dr. Ironside, he said, "Harry, God sold the cattle!"

If we approach God through prayer in an attitude of rejoicing, the Lord will often move heaven on our behalf.

Let's pray:

⊠

Prayer of Praise

Almighty God, your word declares that I should come into your gates with thanksgiving and enter your courts with praise. I want to always be thankful and to bless your holy name.

You alone, O God, are worthy of all praise. I will praise you early in the morning and in the noonday for all of your mighty benefits. Grant me to be a man that is continually filled with your praise that I might be filled with your everlasting joy in every circumstance.

Amen.

⊠

Prayer of Rejoicing

Heavenly Father, I know that the trial of my faith is much more precious than gold or silver which perishes. Though I may be tried by fire, I desire to continue rejoicing and praising your name throughout any situation.

I rejoice in you, O God, and extol all honor unto your name. For you alone are worthy to receive all glory. Because of your everlasting mercy, I can rejoice when I fall in various temptations. I am confident that the trying of my faith is developing patience in me. Bless your name— Almighty God!

Amen.

⊗

Prayer to Rejoice When Things Appear Hopeless

Father God, I come to you because you are my hope of rejoicing—despite my circumstances. I understand there is a distinction between happiness and rejoicing. Happiness, Lord, is fleeting and often depends on situations outside of my control. I can rejoice whether I am happy inside or not.

Right now, Lord, fill me with your hope so that I might bring you glory in the midst of this seemingly hopeless situation. I admit, Lord, I don't see any way out of this situation. Instead, I ask for you to open a door of possibility that at the present time, I can't see. You can fling open this door from what looks like a wall, then alleviate the situation in a fresh way. Thank you, God, that you know and understand the beginning from the end.

Thank you, God, for providing the Spirit of rejoicing and giving that Spirit to me. I will trust in you and rejoice in you as my great God.

Amen.

⊗

BIBLE VERSES ABOUT REJOICING

Create in me a clean heart, O God. Renew a right spirit within me. Do not banish me from your presence, and don't take your Holy Spirit from me. *Restore to me again the joy of your salvation*, and make me willing to obey you. Then I will teach your ways to sinners, and they will return to you. (Psalm 51:10–13, NLT)

Give thanks to the Lord and proclaim his greatness. Let the whole world know what he has done. Sing to him; yes, sing his praises. Tell everyone about his miracles. Exult in his holy name; *O worshipers of the Lord, rejoice!* Search for the Lord and for his strength, and keep on searching. Think of the wonderful works he has done, the miracles, and the judgments he handed down. (1 Chronicles 16:8–12, NLT)

Always be full of joy in the Lord. I say it again—rejoice! Let everyone see that you are considerate in all you do. Remember, the Lord is coming soon. Don't worry about anything; instead, pray about everything. Tell God what you need, and thank him for all he has done. If you do this, you will experience God's peace, which is far more wonderful than the human mind can understand. His peace will guard your hearts and minds as you live in Christ Jesus. (Philippians 4:4–7, NLT)

CHAPTER 17

Prayers of Thanksgiving

⊗

A STORY ABOUT THANKFULNESS

Several years ago, Luis Palau learned about thankfulness in prayer. Luis has preached to twelve million people in some sixty nations. For many years, Dr. Palau groaned when he started the day and his prayers were mostly complaints like, "Lord, here comes another day. I don't feel up to the tasks before me. There are so many temptations. I don't want to lose my temper. Don't let me fail you. Don't let me grieve you. Don't let me dishonor you if an opportunity to witness comes up. . . ." As Dr. Palau categorized his prayers, it had become a series of groaning, moaning, wailing, and pleading.

One day, a coworker Fred Renich challenged Luis and others about prayer. He said, "Most of you probably start out the day groaning. The content, tone, and direction of your prayers are negative." Luis nodded his head in agreement but until then he had not realized the negative tone for his prayers.

Renich was not advocating positive thinking to cure everything. He said, "This is different. Pray on the basis of the promises and reality of God." Then Fred urged his colleagues to start each day with prayers like, "Thank you, Lord Jesus. Here's a new day. Yes, I am weak, but you are strong, and all your resources are my resources. I don't always know how to witness to others, but you will give me the right words. When temptation comes, Lord, I've got your power. Thank you that you live in me. Thank you that your resurrection life is real and that today you're going to prove it once again."

Instead of starting your day with a prayer of unbelief, begin with a note of thanksgiving and praise. Abraham, father of the Jewish people, grew strong in his faith as he gave glory to God. Years before, God had promised Abraham the impossible—that his wife, almost ninety years old, would have a son. The temptation to doubt God's promise must have been incredible. Yet Romans 4:20–21 (NIV) tells us about Abraham: "Yet he did not waver through unbelief regarding the promise of God, but was strengthened in his faith and gave glory to God, being fully persuaded that God had the power to do what He had promised."

Today, let's turn to God in thanksgiving.

Let's pray:

⬦

Prayer of Thanksgiving for Daily Provision

Gracious Father, I want to thank you that you have supplied all of my needs according to your riches in glory by Christ Jesus. How I praise and thank you, Lord, for your rich blessings in my life. Help me to remember that a man's life does not consist in the abundance of physical possessions. Instead my spiritual abundance of life is found in you. I thank you that you know everything that I need before I speak or think the words and that you meet my needs because of your faithfulness. I offer my thanksgiving that you are a God who is more than enough for my every need.

Amen.

⊠

Prayer for Thanksgiving for Health

Mighty God, I thank you for my health and simply my physical well-being. If there is anyone in the Universe who knows me—it's you, God. Thank you for caring so much about my ills and the frailties of my life. Thank you for your healing power and your will that I live in health. How I thank you, God, for your promise that you took my infirmities and carried my sickness. As your Son, Jesus, died on the cross, you redeemed my life from certain destruction and crowned me instead with your loving kindness and tender mercies. You are truly the great physician and the giver of all health. Thank you, Lord.

Amen.

⊠

A Prayer of Thanksgiving for My Family

Father, you've told me in the Bible that I am a high priest and the head of my household. I offer thanks to you for your presence in my home. I thank you, Father, that as the spiritual leader of my home, I can declare on the authority of your Word that my family will be strong and upright. Thank you, Lord, that more than wealth or riches, my family will endure forever. You've told man that only two things endure forever—the Bible and people.

It is with a grateful heart that I approach you today. I reverence you and worship you. In a solemn pledge, I promise that as for me and my house, we will serve the Lord.

Amen.

⊠

Prayer of Thanksgiving for Soundness of Mind

God, you are my Heavenly Father and Protector, and I give you thanks today for a sound mind. I thank you that in Christ Jesus, you have provided a way for me to be free from depression, anxiety, guilt, and worry. I thank you, God, for your confidence that keeps me from being shaken in mind and being troubled in spirit.

Because of my faith in your name and your word, I have been given perfect soundness of mind, soul, and body. Thank you, God, for the grace that you have given to me to experience total wholeness. I thank you that the Scriptures declare, we are fearful and wonderfully made. Today I rejoice in your goodness.

Amen.

⊠

BIBLE VERSES ABOUT THANKSGIVING

Come, let's sing for joy to the Lord. Let's shout praises to the Rock who saves us. Let's come to him with *thanksgiving*. Let's sing songs to him, because the Lord is the great God, the great King over all gods. The deepest places on earth are his, and the highest mountains belong to him. The sea is his because he made it, and he created the land with his own hands.

Come, let's worship him and bow down. Let's kneel before the Lord who made us, because he is our God and we are the people he takes care of and the sheep that he tends. (Psalm 95:1–7a, NCV)

Shout to the Lord, all the earth. Serve the Lord with joy; come before him with singing. Know that the Lord is God. He made us, and we belong to him; we are his people, the sheep he tends.

Come into his city with songs of thanksgiving and into his courtyards with songs of praise. *Thank* him and praise his name. The Lord is good. His love is forever, and his loyalty goes on and on. (Psalm 100:1–5, NCV)

Be full of joy in the Lord always. I will say again, be full of joy. Let everyone see that you are gentle and kind. The Lord is coming soon.

Do not worry about anything, but pray and ask God for everything you need, always *giving thanks*. And God's peace, which is so great we cannot understand it, will keep your hearts and minds in Christ Jesus. (Philippians 4:4–7, NCV)

Let the peace that Christ gives control your thinking, because you were all called together in one body to have peace. Always be *thankful*.

Let the teaching of Christ live in you richly. Use all wisdom to teach and instruct each other by singing psalms, hymns, and spiritual songs with thankfulness in your hearts to God. Everything you do or say should be done to obey Jesus your Lord. And in all you do, *give thanks* to God the Father through Jesus. (Colossians 3:15–17, NCV)

CHAPTER 18

Prayers for the Changes in Life

⊠

A STORY ABOUT CHANGES IN LIFE

Several years ago, John Wimber, founder of the Vineyard Fellowships, talked with a new Christian about some changes in his life. Harry had made a decision for Christ and much of his life was different. For years, Harry had dropped by the same bar every day after work—more for the friendship than for the beer.

The next Monday, Harry walked into the bar as usual and his friends asked, "How is it going?" Harry ordered a beer and proceeded to describe for them how he gave his life to Jesus Christ. Suddenly his friends lapsed into a stony silence and Harry began to feel uncomfortable and out of place. Over the next day or two, Harry noticed that the cigarette smoke bothered him for the first time, the beer didn't taste as good as it used to, and the coarse language was suddenly foreign to him. By midweek, Harry realized he no longer belonged in the bar. As he talked with John Wimber, Harry wanted to understand how everything could change so rapidly and drastically.

"That's easy," John said. "You're a new man, with a new heart and desires. You'll never enjoy the old life again."

The changes in your life might not be so radical but each of us experiences change. We locate a new job. We move to a new home. We start a new relationship. Children enter the home where there were only a husband and wife. Or people pass in and out of our circle of close friends. How do you handle these changes in your life? One answer is to turn to a force which is always constant and always available. In the midst of change, the Lord can understand and ease the trauma of change. In these prayers, we ask for God's enabling, strength, and involvement in the midst of change. He can be the constancy in your life.

Let's pray:

⬦

Prayer for Calmness in the Swirl of Life

God, change confronts me at every turn. In this world, change seems to drive everything. I seem to get one aspect of my life in order then another part of it rears its head for attention. In the midst of the uncertainty of change, I ask for your peace and calmness to fill my life and heart.

As I think about the heavens, there is a consistency in the rising and setting of the sun. It never changes. Throughout a single year, the seasons shift from winter to spring to summer to fall—without changing. You set these seasons into motion and you set the earth to revolve around the sun. Thank you that these characteristics demonstrate your unchanging and unfailing love toward us.

As relationships change, and aspects of my work and family life, I want to commit these changes into your capable hands. I ask for you to help me to be a calming and gentle influence to others when they are facing uncertainty from change. I turn the control of today over to you and thank you in advance for your peace in the swirl of change.

Amen.

⊠

Prayer for Moving to a New Location

Lord, I submit to your wisdom and direction concerning myself (and my family) for moving to a new location. I ask, Lord, for you to go before us to make the crooked places straight as we find a new place to live.

Father, I commit this move into your capable hands. I trust you to provide all that is needed regarding this change in my life—from finances to new friends to a new house of worship to the perfect location.

Grant me the wisdom to make the necessary decisions with everyone involved in this move. Help me to keep my mind focused on you so I might experience the peace which passes all understanding. Thank you, Lord, for your loving kindness. I trust in you and acknowledge your guiding hand. I have total confidence that you will direct my steps.

Amen.

⊠

Prayer for the Newly Married

Dear Heavenly Father, I love my new wife, as Christ loves the Church. I have surrendered myself totally to her so I can love, nourish, carefully protect, and cherish her.

I pray that our marriage will be honorable and bring glory to you. Please help our marriage grow stronger each day in our bond of unity. Help us to turn to the Bible for our source of wisdom and to daily keep our lives firmly in your love.

Thank you, Father, that you are knitting us together in truth, making us perfect for every good work. May you watch over our new marriage. Then our relationship as a couple will be seen as a light which shines clearly to the world.

Amen.

Prayer for New Employment and/or a Promotion

Lord God, I want to thank you for your provision of my new job (or my promotion). The Bible tells us that you are the giver of every good and perfect gift. I want to acknowledge and recognize that this promotion doesn't come from my own energy or strength but it comes from you and your action in my life.

May I be productive and demonstrate your character throughout this day. Lord, strengthen me for the work that you have called me to do and let not my hands become weak. I commit this new employment to you and I praise you for your marvelous love.

Lord, I ask that my work will be rewarding and fruitful. Please help me, Lord, to model my life after Christ. Then other people will be able to see my work and glorify you for how you continually work in my life.

Amen.

⬦

Prayer for the Birth of Children

Gracious God, I know that every child is a precious gift of your creation. Bless my child with the awareness of your active presence and involvement in their life. I welcome this new baby into our home and family.

While we rejoice in this new life, we also want to recognize that this new presence is going to change our family forever. We ask for your special touch and strength as we face the multitude of differences in our daily living. We can't handle these changes on our own strength but want to totally cast ourselves in your capable hands for every decision and every change in life.

I praise you, Father, for this special creation. I ask that you would grant good health to this child and even now strengthen him/her. May this child grow to know your love and walk with you all of the days of his/her life.

Thank you, God, for blessing me with ———. I dedicate ———'s life to you. Give me the wisdom that I need to be a loving father. Lord, send friends into my life that will assist me with wisdom, prayers, and encouragement which I'm sure I will need from time to time. Thank you for your incredible provision and the riches that you bless us in Christ Jesus.

Amen.

⬦

BIBLE VERSES ABOUT THE CHANGES IN LIFE

Ever since I first heard of your strong faith in the Lord Jesus and your love for Christians everywhere, I have never stopped thanking God for you. I pray for you constantly, asking God, the glorious Father of our Lord Jesus Christ, to give you spiritual wisdom and understanding, so that you might grow in your knowledge of God.

I pray that your hearts will be flooded with light so that you can understand the wonderful future he has promised to those he called. I want you to realize what a rich and glorious inheritance he has given to his people. I pray that you will begin to understand the incredible greatness of his power for us who believe him. This is the same mighty power that raised Christ from the dead and seated him in the place of honor at God's right hand in the heavenly realms. (Ephesians 1:15–20, NLT)

"For I know the plans I have for you," says the Lord. "They are plans for good and not for disaster, to give you a future and a hope. In those days when you pray, I will listen. If you look for me in earnest, you will find me when you seek me." (Jeremiah 29:11–13, NLT)

My child, how I will rejoice if you become wise. Yes, my heart will thrill when you speak what is right and just. Don't envy sinners, but always continue to fear the Lord. For surely you have a future ahead of you; your hope will not be disappointed. My child, listen and be wise. Keep your heart on the right course. (Proverbs 23:15–19, NLT)

CHAPTER 19

Prayers for Your Future

⬦

A STORY ABOUT THE FUTURE

Each of us has dreams and plans for the future. As Dudley Hall described in *Grace Works*, our plans and God's plans are not always one and the same. As a high-school senior, Hall yielded his life to Christian ministry and chose to attend a private denominational university to prepare for his life's vocation. In addition, Hall received a football scholarship and his constant prayer was, "Lord, help me to be a good football player, and I will use that athlete's platform to speak for you."

Dudley thought he and God had struck a deal. As God helped Hall be a successful athlete, then he would in turn talk with God to football-smitten young people. During his freshman year, Hall started on the team and showed great promise. In the final game of the season, Dudley was blocked from behind and suffered a fractured hip. After lying immobile in the hospital for several weeks, his doctor told him that he would never play football again.

Dudley was devastated because he couldn't keep his promise to God! As he said, "What kind of hero is a crippled freshman?"

While Hall thought God wanted him to be a football hero who could put in a good word about God to young people, in reality, God wanted to direct Hall's future plans. He recalls the day alone in hospital room 101 when he prayed, "O God, I can't do anything you wanted me to do!" Then in his spirit, Hall heard God's reply—"I love you just like you are. I don't want a hero. I just want you." That day, Dudley gained a broader understanding of God's direction for his future life. God can be trusted to direct the steps for our future. We need to be active in prayer and involving God in our future plans—instead of planning on our own energy, then asking for God's blessing.

Let's pray:

⊗

Prayer for the Hope of Your Future

Lord Jesus, you are the hope of my future. You have given me hope of an inheritance that is undefiled and incorruptible. You have also declared that my inheritance will never fade away. Help me, I pray, Lord, to hold fast to the confidence that I have in you and your plans for my life and future. My faith and hope are completely in you and I rest knowing that your thoughts for me are for good and not for evil. Because of this great hope which resides in my heart, I can face the future with full assurance and faith in you.

Amen.

⊠

Prayer to be Equipped for Future Success

Heavenly Father, I know that success requires faithfulness in the little things. I pray, Dear God, that I may learn then do all that you have written in your word. Then you will make my way prosperous and you will give me good success. Lord, I believe it is your desire for me to succeed. Help me to learn to measure success according to the standards of your words in the Bible instead of the world's standard. Help me to fulfill your law and to be found faithful in all of my responsibilities. As I am faithful in these responsibilities, then I will owe no man anything and my only debt will be to love you, God. I know that I will be equipped with success in my future as I surrender my will and daily actions to you. Lord, I thank you for equipping me.

Amen.

⊠

Prayer to Wait on God's Direction for My Future

Almighty God, my soul waits silently for you and you alone. I pray that I will wait on you for my future direction. God, waiting is so hard but I pray for you to renew my strength during this period of my life. Hear my prayer and help me to wait patiently on you. O Lord, I don't want to be an independent man but I want to continue in the same direction that you want for my life. I want to be a man who is dependent on you. Help me not to be my own leader but to follow you as my leader.

Thank you for opening my eyes to the fact that I am your child. You are in control of the direction for my future. Thank you, Gracious Lord, for your patience with me.

Amen.

◇

BIBLE VERSES ABOUT THE FUTURE

I waited patiently for the Lord. He turned to me and heard my cry. He lifted me out of the pit of destruction, out of the sticky mud. He stood me on a rock and made my feet steady.

He put a new song in my mouth, a song of praise to our God. Many people will see this and worship him. Then they will trust the Lord. Happy is the person who trusts the Lord, who doesn't turn to those who are proud or to those who worship false gods.

Lord my God, you have done many miracles. *Your plans for us are many*. If I tried to tell them all, there would be too many to count. You do not want sacrifices and offerings. But you have made a hole in my ear to show that my body and life are yours. You do not ask for burnt offerings and sacrifices to take away sins.

Then I said, "Look, I have come. It is written about me in the book. My God, I want to do what you want. Your teachings are in my heart." (Psalm 40:1–8, NCV)

My child, if you are wise, then I will be happy. I will be so pleased if you speak what is right. Don't envy sinners, but always respect the Lord. *Then you will have hope for the future*, and your wishes will come true.

Listen, my child, and be wise. Keep your mind on what is right. (Proverbs 23:15–19, NCV)

• • •

The followers were amazed at what Jesus said. But he said again, "My children, it is very hard to enter the kingdom of God! It is easier for a camel to go through the eye of a needle than for a rich person to enter the kingdom of God."

The followers were even more surprised and said to each other, "Then who can be saved?"

Jesus looked at them and said, "This is something people cannot do, but God can. God can do all things."

Peter said to Jesus, "Look, we have left everything and followed you."

Jesus said, "I tell you the truth, all those who have left houses, brothers, sisters, mother, father, children, or farms for me and for the Good News will get more than they left. Here in this world they will have a hundred times more homes, brothers, sisters, mothers, children, and fields. And with those things, they will also suffer for their belief. But in the age that is coming they will have life forever.

"*Many who have the highest place now will have the lowest place in the future. And many who have the lowest place now will have the highest place in the future.*" (Mark 10:24–31, NCV)

Dear friends, now we are children of God, and we have not yet been shown what we will be in the future. But we know that *when Christ comes again, we will be like him,* because we will see him as he really is. Christ is pure, and all who have this hope in Christ keep themselves pure like Christ.

The person who sins breaks God's law. Yes, sin is living against God's law. You know that Christ came to take away sins and that there is no sin in Christ. So anyone who lives in Christ does not go on sinning. Anyone who goes on sinning has never really understood Christ and has never known him.

Dear children, do not let anyone lead you the wrong way. Christ is all that is right. So to be like Christ a person must do what is right. (1 John 3:2–7, NCV)

CHAPTER 20

Prayers for Repentance
of Wrongdoing

◇

A STORY ABOUT REPENTANCE

J. C. Penney was known to be honest and a good man. It wasn't until his later years of life that he became interested in spiritual matters. His early years were focused on success and making money. Looking back on his life, he says, "When I worked for six dollars a week at Joslin's Dry Goods Store in Denver, it was my ambition, in the sense of wealth in money, to be worth one hundred thousand dollars. When I reached that goal, I felt a certain temporary satisfaction, but it soon wore off and my sights were set on becoming worth a million dollars."

Mr. and Mrs. Penney worked hard to expand the business, then one day Mrs. Penney caught cold and pneumonia developed. Suddenly she died. It was through his wife's death J. C. Penney understood money was a poor substitute for the real purposes of living.

"When she died, my world crashed about me. To build a business, to make a success in the eyes of men, to accumulate money—

what was the purpose of life? What had money meant to my wife? I felt mocked by life, even by God Himself!" In the months ahead, Penney passed through several financial trials which left him in ruin and deep distress. During these days, God dealt with his self-righteous nature and his love of money. Penney turned to God in repentance. He said, "I had to pass through fiery ordeals before reaching glimmerings of conviction that it is not enough for men to be upright and moral. When I was brought to humility and the knowledge of the repentance to God in prayer, a light illumined my being. I can not otherwise describe it than to say it changed me as a man forever."

As men, we can turn to God with sincerity and repentance from our past. Because God sees the beginning and the end of our days, the Heavenly Father reaches to us in his mercy and love, then takes a man into eternity.

Let's pray:

⊠

Prayer of Repentance for Not Living a Life of Purity

Gracious God, you know that as a man, I have been enticed into the wisdom of the world instead of the Bible. I have lived and acted according to the dictates of my sensual nature and I have not followed the truth in the Bible.

I don't want to follow the craving of my sensual desires. You, O God, are rich in mercy even with my short-comings and sin. Father, by your grace, I have been saved and my salvation is very special to me. Now, since I am in Christ and you have given me a new nature and declared me a new creation, I desire to be free from all impurities and deceit. Father, I choose to be a man who is chaste and undefiled. Please lead me in the paths of righteousness for your namesake.

Thank you, God, for granting me your power that is at work within me.

Amen.

⊠

Prayer of Repentance for Not Living a Life of Integrity

Lord, you want me to be a man of integrity. Scripture declares that the integrity of the upright shall guide them; but the perseverance of the sinner will destroy them.

Father, I repent of not living consistently a life of integrity in my heart. My actions might not show to the average person but I know the wrong intentions of my heart and how I've stretched the truth. Lord, help me to be like Christ and to live as a man who refuses to abandon his integrity in the middle of any difficult situation. Redeem me and, Lord, be merciful to me, I pray. Help me to be a man who will model integrity for other men. Give me the grace to protect and guard my heart with all diligence. Permit integrity and uprightness of actions to uphold my life because I wait on you, gracious God.

Amen.

⊠

Prayer of Repentance for Complaining

Father, I repent for giving place to complaining. In our world, it so easy to tear down situations and find fault with other people—instead of encouraging and helping other people. I recognize that I've been selfish and centered on my own comfort instead of others'. I've allowed that selfish desire to drive my actions and the words from my mouth. These words have become complaints and dissatisfaction.

As a man who is in the service of the Eternal God, I want to do all things without murmuring and disputing. Lord, when I am agitated, I ask for your assistance and protection to stop my complaining. Help me to move through life with a great sense of your guidance and peace. Then help me to transfer that peace to others—especially when they are complaining. Through my calm response, use these actions to draw other people to yourself and your life.

Lord, whenever I tend to fall toward complaining and grumbling about a particular situation, help me to turn and consider your benefits and blessings in my life. I want to be diligent in my thankful heart for your grace in my life. It's only through your grace and love that I can have a relationship with you.

O God, help me to stay positive in the middle of difficult situations and allow me to bring my every thought captive to your word and control. From my positive attitude, give me the ability to encourage others and transfer peace to situations which could easily degenerate into complaining and grumbling. The Bible says that blessed are the peacemakers for they will see God. I ask for the ability to be a peacemaker instead of a complainer.

Today, I pray believing that you will give me this desire.

Amen.

⊠

BIBLE VERSES ABOUT REPENTANCE

So Samuel called to the Lord, and the Lord sent thunder and rain. And all the people were terrified of the Lord and of Samuel. "Pray to the Lord your God for us, or we will die!" they cried out to Samuel. "For now we have added to our sins by asking for a king."

"Don't be afraid," Samuel reassured them. "You have certainly done wrong, but make sure now that you worship the Lord with all your heart and that you don't turn your back on him in any way. Don't go back to worshiping worthless idols that cannot help or rescue you—they really are useless!

"The Lord will not abandon his chosen people, for that would dishonor his great name. He made you a special nation for himself. As for me, I will certainly not sin against the Lord by ending my prayers for you. And I will continue to teach you what is good and right. But be sure to fear the Lord and sincerely worship him. Think of all the wonderful things he has done for you. (1 Sam 12:18–24, NLT)

Seek the Lord while you can find him. Call on him now while he is near. Let the people turn from their wicked deeds. Let them banish from their minds the very thought of doing wrong! Let them turn to the Lord that he may have mercy on them. Yes, turn to our God, for he will abundantly pardon.

"My thoughts are completely different from yours," says the Lord. "And my ways are far beyond anything you could imagine. For just as the heavens are higher than the earth, so are my ways higher than your ways and my thoughts higher than your thoughts." (Isaiah 55:6–9, NLT)

• • •

"Jeremiah, say to the people, 'This is what the Lord says: When people fall down, don't they get up again? When they start down the wrong road and discover their mistake, don't they turn back?' "

Then why do these people keep going along their self-destructive path, refusing to turn back, even though I have warned them? I listen to their conversations, and what do I hear? Is anyone sorry for sin? Does anyone say, "What a terrible thing I have done?" No! All are running down the path of sin as swiftly as a horse rushing into battle!

The stork knows the time of her migration, as do the turtledove, the swallow, and the crane. They all return at the proper time each year. But not my people! They do not know what the Lord requires of them. (Jeremiah 8:4–7, NLT)

Then I will teach your ways to those who do wrong, and sinners will turn back to you. God, save me from the guilt of murder, God, of my salvation, and I will sing about your goodness.

Lord, let me speak so I may praise you. You are not pleased by sacrifices, or I would give them. You don't want burnt offerings. The sacrifice God wants is a broken spirit. God, you will not reject a heart that is broken and sorry for sin. (Psalm 51:13–17, NCV)

CHAPTER 21

Prayers for Restoration in Broken Relationships

⊠

A STORY ABOUT BROKEN RELATIONSHIPS

By his nature, Tom's father was a highly critical, unhappy man. Even when Tom earned a Ph.D., he didn't gain much attention from his father. When Tom married, his father never quite accepted his wife, often severely criticizing her. As the years passed, one day Tom's father died. He always regretted that he never talked through his feelings with his dad and was reconciled. The relationship was broken forever. The pain mounted when his brothers told Tom that their dad had written him out of his will and never told him.

After months of feeling depressed, Tom sat down one day and wrote his father a long letter. A few days later, he slid behind the steering wheel early in the morning and drove the long journey to an adjoining state where his father was buried. After several hours of grief alone, Tom pulled out a letter to his father from his pocket. He placed the letter on top of his father's tomb and then burned it. As the flames licked the paper, Tom hoped his pain would disappear. Today, if you asked Tom, he would tell you that he has a constant regret about the broken relationship with his father. Some kinds of pain never completely disappear.

As Patrick Morley writes in *The Seven Seasons of a Man's Life*, "Some unresolved issues relate to tasks, but by far the majority deal with relationships. In the process we wound and damage the feelings of our loved ones. Remorse goes unexpressed. Forgiveness is not sought. Relationships break down."

Whether you've experienced a broken relationship with a parent, a child, a spouse, or a friend, there is a place which can work like balm on an open wound—prayer with your Heavenly Father. God saw the beginning and the end of your relationship. He can ease your pain through prayer.

Let's pray:

⊠

Prayer for Restoration of the Broken Relationship

God of Heaven, I ask you to restore my broken relationship with ———. I pray that your love would abound in this relationship and that both of us would listen to your voice then respond. Lord, I ask you to overturn all that Satan has meant for evil and the destruction of this relationship. Thank you that the Bible tells us that you work everything together for good with those who love Christ Jesus and who are called according to his purpose. Please work out this broken relationship for your good and your purpose.

Lord, search my own heart as I consider my relationship with ———. If I have done anything to cause this relationship to crumble, then shine your light of truth into my heart and reveal it to me. Help me to approach ——— in the spirit of reconciliation and restoration. I ask that you cut out any bitterness in my heart about my relationship with ———. The book of Hebrews tells us that a root of bitterness, if left, can fester and cause many difficulties in the days ahead. I ask that you would remove the smallest strain of bitterness so that our relationship can be restored and healed.

You, God, are more than able to work in this particular situation. I thank you that nothing is too hard for you. Thank you for loving us enough to move in this relationship for your glory.

Amen.

◇

Prayer for Freedom from Bitterness

Heavenly Father, because of this relationship with ———, I have become a bitter man. This bitterness is spilling over into my other relationships and my overall countenance. The Bible tells us that we can be free from resentment and bitterness as we turn in prayer to you and your Grace.

Lord, I confess that this bitterness has defiled my life and is destroying it. Release me from the bitterness that has entered my soul. Father, I desire to put away all bitterness, wrath, and anger. I seek to be a tenderhearted man who forgives others easily and without bitterness. Thank you, God, for forgiving me of this bitterness and surrounding me with your Spirit and love.

Amen.

◇

Prayer for Forgiveness

Lord, I understand the truth that because you have forgiven me, I should also seek to forgive others. I want to forgive others as you have forgiven me. Today, I forgive ———— who has caused a breach in our relationship. Please enable me to forgive as much as needed and then even more. I understand that the strength and ability to forgive comes from you and a heart which is centered on your desire to love other people. Fill me with your love toward ————. In your name release grace in my relationship with ———— and help me to bear with him/her when they wrong me. Teach me to be a man who follows in your steps and forgives others.

Amen.

◇

Prayer to Live in Love

Father, I acknowledge that you are the source of love and that you are, in fact, love. I ask for your forgiveness because I am a man who lacks love for others. Help me to always remember that I am able to love others only because you have first loved me. The Bible tells us that you loved the world so much that you gave up your only Son, Jesus Christ, that he would carry the sins of the world and restore our relationship with you.

I want to love other people in the same manner that you have loved me—at a great sacrifice and at all cost. Help me to be a man who lives in faith, hope, and love, then to carry out that love in all of my relationships. I want to thank you in advance for the guiding force of your love in my life.

Amen.

⊠

Prayer of Repentance for My Failure to Turn to God

Father, today I repent of the sin of rebellion. I have failed to turn everything in my life over to you. Yes, I may have turned it over at one time, but then almost immediately I took those situations back on my own shoulders. I'm asking for your forgiveness for trying to manipulate situations on my own strength and energy.

Jesus told us that we should release our burdens into your hands, then you will give us rest and restore us from our sinful past. Help me to live every minute of every day in a way which is pleasing to you. From this day forward, I surrender everything to you!

Amen.

⊠

BIBLE VERSES ABOUT BROKEN RELATIONSHIPS

If at that time you return to the Lord your God, and you and your children begin wholeheartedly to obey all the commands I have given you today, then the Lord your God will restore your fortunes. *He will have mercy on you and gather you back from all the nations where he has scattered you.*

Though you are at the ends of the earth, the Lord your God will go and find you and bring you back again. He will return you to the land that belonged to your ancestors, and you will possess that land again. He will make you even more prosperous and numerous than your ancestors! The

Lord your God will cleanse your heart and the hearts of all your descendants so that you will love him with all your heart and soul, and so you may live! (Deuteronomy 30:2–6, NLT)

You have allowed me to suffer much hardship, but *you will restore me* to life again and lift me up from the depths of the earth. You will restore me to even greater honor and comfort me once again.

Then I will praise you with music on the harp, because you are faithful to your promises, O God. I will sing for you with a lyre, O Holy One of Israel. I will shout for joy and sing your praises, for you have redeemed me. I will tell about your righteous deeds all day long, for everyone who tried to hurt me has been shamed and humiliated. (Psalm 71:20–24, NLT)

Then Peter came to him and asked, "Lord, how often should I forgive someone who sins against me? Seven times?"

"No!" Jesus replied, "seventy times seven!

"For this reason, the Kingdom of Heaven can be compared to a king who decided to bring his accounts up to date with servants who had borrowed money from him. In the process, one of his debtors was brought in who owed him millions of dollars. He couldn't pay, so the king ordered that he, his wife, his children, and everything he had be sold to pay the debt. But the man fell down before the king and begged him, 'Oh, sir, be patient with me, and I will pay it all.'

"Then the king was filled with pity for him, and he released him and forgave his debt.

"But when the man left the king, he went to a fellow servant who owed him a few thousand dollars. He grabbed him by the throat and demanded instant payment. His fellow servant fell down before him and begged for a little more time. 'Be patient and I will pay it,' he pleaded.

"But his creditor wouldn't wait. He had the man arrested and jailed until the debt could be paid in full. When some of the other servants saw this, they were very upset. They went to the king and told him what had happened. Then the king called in the man he had forgiven and said, 'You evil servant! I forgave you that tremendous debt because you pleaded with me. Shouldn't you have mercy on your fellow servant, just as I had mercy on you?' Then the angry king sent the man to prison until he had paid every penny.

"That's what my heavenly Father will do to you if you refuse to forgive your brothers and sisters in your heart." (Matthew 18:21–35, NLT)

Be careful! Watch out for attacks from the Devil, your great enemy. He prowls around like a roaring lion, looking for some victim to devour. Take a firm stand against him, and be strong in your faith. Remember that Christians all over the world are going through the same kind of suffering you are.

In his kindness God called you to his eternal glory by means of Jesus Christ. After you have suffered a little while, he will restore, support, and strengthen you, and he will place you on a firm foundation. All power is his forever and ever. Amen. (1 Peter 5:8–11, NLT)

CHAPTER 22

Prayers for Wisdom and Insight

⬦

A Story About Wisdom and Insight

As the chairman of I. M. Group, Ltd., Robert N. Edmiston understands the necessity of turning to God for wisdom and insight. He attributes his success in business to his relationship with God. One of his old bosses told him, "It's not the length of experience that counts, it's the intensity." As he explains, "You can work fifty years filing papers and learn nothing, or you can work six months in an intense situation and learn a tremendous amount."

While working for Jensen Cars as the financial controller, Edmiston's company went through trauma. Within nine months, the company went bankrupt and his career took a sudden nosedive. "God was able to snatch victory out of that, and it became my best learning experience," he says. "After the bankruptcy, I formed a little company called Jensen Parts and Service. From there, with ten thousand dollars, we built a company in seventeen years which was recently valued at something like $450 million."

For his success, Edmiston says he turned to God in daily prayer for each decision—large and small: "Jesus Christ is very much involved with both my life and my business. It is as if He were my senior partner."

Today, you may feel at the end of your rope in a particular situation or relationship. You've tried your best but no solution is forthcoming. Let's approach the Father of all wisdom and insight for a solution.

Let's pray:

◇

A Request for Wisdom

Thank you, God, for the Bible tells us that if any man lacks wisdom, let him ask you, God—and you will generously give wisdom to all men without finding fault. I pray, God, that you would grant me knowledge, instruction, and understanding.

I pray, Lord, that you will fill me with the spirit of wisdom so that I might be able to discern your will and in all my ways become pleasing and fruitful in every good work. By wisdom, you founded the earth and by knowledge you established the heaven.

Establish me, O God, in your wisdom.

I thank you, God, for the Holy Spirit, who permanently abides in me and who guides me into all the truth. Help me, Lord, to walk in your wisdom that is pure, peaceable, gentle and easy to understand, then I can bring you glory with my life. Thank you, Lord, for your promise of wisdom to me in my life.

Amen.

⊠

Prayer for Insight

Dear God, I pray that you would give me your insight and that my understanding would be enlightened. Your words in the Bible declare that I have received not the spirit of the world but your Spirit so that I might have insight and knowledge of the things that have been freely given to me in Christ Jesus.

Help me, God, and enlighten me to know your mighty power and exceedingly great riches. Help me to see beyond my present situation and to acknowledge your sovereignty. You are the one who is in control of the stars in the Heavens and the details of my daily life.

Your word, Lord, is a lamp to my feet and a light to my path. Help me to walk in the light as you are in the light. Your light brings insight and leads me to you, brightening my life and purifying my soul. I look to you, O Lord, for insight and I will wait for you to bring me salvation.

I pray, God, that you will keep me walking in your light because you are the one and only true light that illuminates the steps of every man in the world. The light of your life will sustain me as I wait patiently on you.

Amen.

⊠

A Protective Prayer for Discernment

Father, there are so many competing voices in my world. Whether it's the car radio or the television set or my newspaper, information seems to barrage me everywhere. I need your guidance about this information. Help me to watch or listen to the things which are pleasing in your sight. And for these other voices which do not come from your hand? Help me to turn off the radio, avoid a particular newspaper article, or simply change the television channel. I pray that you will protect my mind and give me your discernment about such matters. I confess my weakness in this area. It's all too easy, Lord, to permit the noise to continue and then try to find wisdom in something which is rooted in foolishness.

God, I have to live in this world but teach me how to not be a part of it. Give me a sense of balance and a proper perspective on these competing voices. Give me time in prayer to discover your still, small voice. I recall the story of Elijah who wanted to hear your voice. It was not in the fire or the wind but in the whispered voice. Thank you, God, for that lesson and help me to apply it into my life today.

Amen.

◇

Prayer for Guidance to Wise Counsel

Lord, every day seems full of a multitude of decisions— large and small. In the case of the large ones and the small ones, I ask for you to guide me to wise truth. While the principles in the Bible are eternal, the specifics for my modern world are not always in those pages. For example, how do I know which vehicle to purchase or which job to take or where to live? I pray that you will bring wise counselors into my life. I ask you to go before me and prepare the way for my buying decisions and everyday living decisions.

I ask you, Lord, to give me a spiritual hunger and a thirst for knowledge about you. As I spend time reading the Bible, use those words and lessons as I live in this modern world. Help me to apply those lessons in fresh ways.

Move godly people into my life who can help me make wise decisions. Give me a wise older man who can mentor and teach me about your ways of life. Then help me have a friend who is closer than a brother where I can bear my heart and gain wisdom and insight. Finally, God, give me someone like Paul had Timothy—a younger man where I can teach and impart the wise lessons that you have taught me. I ask for these special "counselors" to be brought into my life on your timetable. In advance, I thank you for the blessing from these other men.

Amen.

⊗

BIBLE VERSES ABOUT WISDOM AND INSIGHT

That night the Lord appeared to Solomon in a dream, and God said, "What do you want? Ask, and I will give it to you!"

Solomon replied, "You were wonderfully kind to my father, David, because he was honest and true and faithful to you. And you have continued this great kindness to him today by giving him a son to succeed him. O Lord my God, now you have made me king instead of my father, David, but I am like a little child who doesn't know his way around.

"And here I am among your own chosen people, a nation so great they are too numerous to count! *Give me an understanding mind* so that I can govern your people well and know the difference between right and wrong. For who by himself is able to govern this great nation of yours?"

The Lord was pleased with Solomon's reply and was glad that he had asked for wisdom. So God replied, "Because you have asked for wisdom in governing my people and have not asked for a long life or riches for yourself or the death of your enemies—I will give you what you asked for! I will give you a wise and understanding mind such as no one else has ever had or ever will have! And I will also give you what you did not ask for—riches and honor! No other king in all the world will be compared to you for the rest of your life! (1 Kings 3:5–13, NLT)

Oh, what a wonderful God we have! How great are his riches and *wisdom and knowledge*! How impossible it is for us to understand his decisions and his methods! For who can know what the Lord is thinking? Who knows enough to be his counselor? And who could ever give him so much that he would have to pay it back?

For everything comes from him; everything exists by his power and is intended for his glory. To him be glory evermore. Amen. (Romans 11:33–36, NLT)

Stop fooling yourselves. If you think you are *wise* by this world's standards, you will have to become a fool so you can become wise by God's standards. For *the wisdom of this world is foolishness to God*. As the Scriptures say, "God catches those who think they are wise in their own cleverness."

And again, "The Lord knows the thoughts of the wise, that they are worthless." (1 Corinthians 3:18–20, NLT)

So we have continued praying for you ever since we first heard about you. We ask God to give you a complete understanding of what he wants to do in your lives, and *we ask him to make you wise with spiritual wisdom*. Then the way you live will always honor and please the Lord, and you will continually do good, kind things for others. All the while, you will learn to know God better and better.

We also pray that you will be strengthened with his glorious power so that you will have all the patience and endurance you need. May you be filled with joy, always thanking the Father, who has enabled you to share the inheritance that belongs to God's holy people, who live in the light. (Colossians 1:9–12, NLT)

If you need *wisdom*—if you want to know what God wants you to do—ask him, and he will gladly tell you. He will not resent your asking.

But when you ask him, be sure that you really expect him to answer, for a doubtful mind is as unsettled as a wave of the sea that is driven and tossed by the wind. People like that should not expect to receive anything from the Lord. They can't make up their minds. They waver back and forth in everything they do. Christians who are poor should be glad, for God has honored them. (James 1:5–9, NLT)

CHAPTER 23

Prayers for Unanswered Situations

⊠

A Story About an Unanswered Situation

While each of us would like to have God instantly answer our prayers—as we would like them answered—it does not happen in many circumstances. Accidents and illnesses—especially with tiny children—raise the most-unanswered questions. With our voice turned to heaven, we shout, "Why, God?" And the only response is silence.

Pastor Ron Mehl tells the story of another unanswered situation in *God Works the Night Shift* when a young wife grew gravely ill, then suddenly died. Her big husband and flaxen-haired four-year-old girl were left behind. After the funeral service, neighbors gathered around and someone offered, "Please bring your little girl and stay with us for several days. You shouldn't go back home just yet."

Although he was broken-hearted, the man answered, "Thank you, friends, for the kind offer. But we need to go back home—where she was. My baby and I must face this." So the pair returned home to what looked like an empty and lifeless house. The father carried his daughter's little bed into his bedroom so they could face the first dark night together.

This first night, the little girl was having a difficult time trying to sleep . . . and so was her father. Nothing pierced the heart of the man more than hearing his child sobbing for a mother who would never return.

Long into the night, the little one continued to weep. As he reached into her bed, the man tried to comfort her as best he could. Finally she managed to stop crying, but only out of sorrow for her father. Thinking that his daughter was asleep, he looked up and said brokenly, "I trust you, Father, but . . . it's as dark as midnight!"

After hearing her dad's prayer, the little girl began to cry again. "I thought you were asleep, baby," he said.

"Papa, I did try. I was sorry for you. I did try. But—I couldn't go to sleep. Papa, did you ever know it could be so dark? Why, Papa? I can't even see you, it's so dark." Then, through her tears, the little girl whispered, "But you love me even if it's dark—don't you, Papa? You love me even if I don't see you, don't you, Papa?"

For an answer, the big man reached across with his massive hands, lifted his girl out of bed, brought her over onto his chest, and held her, until at last she fell asleep. When she was finally quiet, he began to pray. He took his little daughter's cry to him, and passed it up to God.

"Father . . . it's dark as midnight. I can't see you at all. But you love me, even when it's dark and I can't see you, don't you?"

Today you may feel like your world has gone completely black through an unanswered situation. We can talk with the God of all comfort about our fears and struggles—asking for his light and love to flood our hearts.

Let's pray:

◇

Prayer for an Unanswered Situation

OGracious Father, I praise you for your great faithfulness. I realize that delays are not always denial. I have sought you, Lord, and I know that you have heard me. I confess to you that I need to enter into your rest in this situation. Your word declares that there is a rest for a man where he can cease from his works.

Keep me, O God, I pray, from trying so hard in my own strength that I fail to trust you. Help me to trust in you, Lord, with all my heart and to not lean on my own understanding but in all my ways to acknowledge you.

As I trust you, Father, I will continue in prayer and supplication. I know that you alone, O God, will grant me the sufficiency that I need for this situation. Because my heart is fixed in trusting you, I do not have to be afraid of any evil tidings.

Thank you, Lord, for reassuring me that you are working your purposes out in my life and that you are the master of all circumstances. I resolve never to lose sight of the precious promise from the Bible, that *all things work together for good to them that love God*, to them who are called according to your purpose. Thank you, God, for loving me!

Amen.

◇

Prayer When God Seems Silent

God, I cry out to you today. I've been praying about ———. Over and over I come into your presence and talk with you about this situation. I've been praying for your will yet I don't seem to get any direction or answers from you.

Like the prophets of old and many others throughout the Bible, I cry out to you. Why are you silent? I'll admit that your lack of response is frustrating. It places me on a bit of unsure ground because I don't know which direction to move. Waiting seems impossible but if this is your will and plan for this situation, then please give me the grace and strength to wait.

Even though I've admitted my frustration, I want to thank you today for your faithfulness in my life. I recommit myself to remain faithful to you in prayer about this situation with ———— in spite of your silence. The Bible tells me that you will not give us beyond what we can bear. You must see some inner strength inside that I cannot see in myself. I will continue to pray and trust you to respond in your timing. Thank you that your timing is perfect.

Amen.

◇

Prayer When the Answer Isn't What We Want

Lord, I confess to you that I'm angry and upset. You want us to come into your presence with honesty so it's with this type of honesty that I'm praying. I've been praying about ————. I've knocked on the doors of heaven through my prayers, but my prayers were not answered in the way that I expected.

I want to reaffirm, Lord, that you are not some sort of genie which can be controlled through prayer. I understand that you are the Sovereign Director of the Universe and you have the big picture of our lives—from the beginning to the end. In this particular situation, I'm confused about what you have in mind since it did not turn out as I planned.

Today, Lord, help me to see how your plans are at work in my life—despite what it looks like on the surface. Renew my faith and strength in you. I acknowledge that your ways and plans are higher and far better than anything I could conceive. So I give this situation into your capable hands and ask for you to align my will and plans with your will and plans.

Amen.

⊠

BIBLE VERSES ABOUT UNANSWERED SITUATIONS

My God, my God, why have you rejected me? You seem far from saving me, far from the words of my groaning. My God, I call to you during the day, but you do not answer. I call at night; I am not silent.

You sit as the Holy One. The praises of Israel are your throne. Our ancestors trusted you; they trusted, and you saved them. They called to you for help and were rescued. They trusted you and were not disappointed. (Psalm 22:1–5, NCV)

O God, whom I praise, don't stand silent and aloof while the wicked slander me and tell lies about me. They are all around me with their hateful words, and they fight against me for no reason. I love them, but they try to destroy me—even as I am praying for them! (Psalm 109:1–4, NLT)

Lord, don't continue to be angry with us; don't remember our sins forever. Please, look at us, because we are your people. Your holy cities are empty like the desert. Jerusalem is like a desert; it is destroyed. Our ancestors worshiped you in our holy and wonderful Temple, but now it has been burned with fire, and all our precious things have been destroyed.

When you see these things, will you hold yourself back from helping us, Lord? Will you be silent and punish us beyond what we can stand?

The Lord says, "I made myself known to people who were not looking for me. I was found by those who were not asking me for help. I said, 'Here I am. Here I am,' to a nation that was not praying to me. All day long I stood ready to accept people who turned against me, but the way they continue to live is not good; they do anything they want to do. Right in front of me they continue to do things that make me angry. They offer sacrifices to their gods in their gardens, and they burn incense on altars of brick. They sit among the graves and spend their nights waiting to get messages from the dead. They eat the meat of pigs, and their pots are full of soup made from meat that is wrong to eat.

"But they tell others, 'Stay away, and don't come near me. I am too holy for you.' These people are like smoke in my nose. Like a fire that burns all the time, they continue to make me angry.

"Look, it is written here before me. I will not be quiet; instead, I will repay you in full. I will punish you for what you have done." (Isaiah 64:9–65:6, NCV)

CHAPTER 24

Prayers of Faith

⬨

A STORY ABOUT FAITH

Dr. Bill Bright, founder of Campus Crusade for Christ, believes that everything about the Christian life is based on faith. Without faith, he says, there is no demonstration of God's love. To illustrate his view, Dr. Bright recounted a time when he was having trouble loving a member of his staff. While he knew God's command to love others, because of inconsistencies in this person's life and personality differences, he found it difficult. As he struggled, Dr. Bright was reminded of 1 Peter 5:7 (TLB) which says, "Let him have all your worries and cares, for he is always thinking about you and watching everything that concerns you."

In prayer, Dr. Bright gave the problem to the Lord and determined to love this coworker in faith. He would act lovingly toward the man to the disregard of his own feelings and in the strength of God's love.

An hour later, Dr. Bright received a letter from this very man, who had no possibility of knowing the direction that Dr. Bright had just decided. In fact, his letter was written the day before. God had foreseen the change that would occur in Bill Bright. That afternoon, Dr. Bright met with the friend and had the most beautiful time of prayer and fellowship that they had ever experienced.

As Dr. Bright writes, "I urge you to make a list of everyone whom you do not like and begin today to love them by faith. Include those people who have hurt you in the past. Pray for them. Ask for eyes to see them as Christ sees them. Act lovingly toward them no matter how you feel. We don't love people because they deserve to be loved—we love them because Christ commands it and empowers us to do so."

Your prayers of faith can reach from your own household to around the globe. Let's take those steps of faith.

Let's pray:

⬦

Prayer for Faith

Father, you told us that if we had the faith of a mustard seed, then we could speak to the mountain and it would jump into the sea. I'll admit I've never had such faith so my faith must be pretty tiny. Today I ask that you would increase my faith and help it to grow. I understand that growing faith doesn't come instantaneously but is a gradual process.

Also I want to pray for some people in my life that are difficult to love. I ask that you will give me the faith, strength, and love for these individuals. It's outside of my capacity and strength to love these individuals. If I love them in my own strength, I'm doomed to fail but in faith, I ask for your enabling to love these people in your strength and power.

Heavenly Father, the mustard seed while tiny can grow into a huge tree which provides shade for the animals and birds of the air. I'm asking for my faith to increase and right now I trust you to act on my behalf.

Amen.

◇

Prayer for Faith to Overcome Obstacles

Lord God, I know that it is faith that gives me that victory to overcome obstacles. Because I have found a personal relationship with you through Jesus Christ, I claim your victory over the outcome. In your hand is power and might and from your hand, you give strength to all. Thank you, God, for giving me the victory in every area of my life.

Forgive me, Lord, for allowing obstacles to defeat my spirit and drag me down. Because of you, God, I can stand steadfast, immovable, and always abounding in the work of the Lord. Thank you, Jesus, for your ability to live in me and help me overcome any obstacle that I face today.

Amen.

◇

Prayer for Faith to Live in Obedience

Father, help me to have the faith that I need to live in obedience to you and the truth in the Bible. It is true that obeying your voice is far better than any sacrifice. Give me the faith, God, to not waiver and to believe in your guiding hand to lead my life.

Forgive me for each time where I have rebelled against you. I repent of all my actions of disobedience and my failure to do what you have commanded in the Bible. O God, I want to obey you. Increase my faith, dear Lord, to obey your word without any hesitation so that I may rest every day in you. Prolong my days so that I may live with you and that it may go well with me.

Amen.

◇

Prayer for Faith to Share the Faith

Dear God, you know that I often struggle with talking about my relationship with you to other people. I ask you to grant me the faith to become a bold witness for you. Many times, God, I sense you prompting me to say something about my spiritual relationship with someone else. However, I often lack the faith to trust you for the words in those moments.

Empower my life, Lord, and I pray that others will ask me about what's different in my life—and that difference is you in me. Lord, give me your heart for the lost and a deeper understanding that without you in their life, they are bound for an eternity away from you. Guide my words and help me to be faithful to this important calling. Give me a compassion for the lost. Thank you in advance, Lord, for the faith to declare your glory and to be your faithful witness to others.

Amen.

◇

BIBLE VERSES ABOUT PRAYERS AND FAITH

"Simon, Simon, Satan has asked to have all of you, to sift you like wheat. *But I have pleaded in prayer for you, Simon, that your faith should not fail.* So when you have repented and turned to me again, strengthen and build up your brothers."

Peter said, "Lord, I am ready to go to prison with you, and even to die with you."

But Jesus said, "Peter, let me tell you something. The rooster will not crow tomorrow morning until you have denied three times that you even know me." (Luke 22:31–34, NLT)

Are any among you sick? They should call for the elders of the church and have them pray over them, anointing them with oil in the name of the Lord. And their prayer offered in faith will heal the sick, and the Lord will make them well. And anyone who has committed sins will be forgiven.

Confess your sins to each other and *pray for each other so that you may be healed. The earnest prayer [prayer in faith] of a righteous person has great power and wonderful results.* Elijah was as human as we are, and yet when he prayed earnestly that no rain would fall, none fell for the next three and a half years! Then he prayed for rain, and down it poured. The grass turned green, and the crops began to grow again. (James 5:14–18, NLT)

How we thank God for you! Because of you we have great joy in the presence of God. *Night and day we pray earnestly for you, asking God to let us see you again to fill up anything that may still be missing in your faith.*

May God himself, our Father, and our Lord Jesus make it possible for us to come to you very soon. And may the Lord make your love grow and overflow to each other and to everyone else, just as our love overflows toward you.

As a result, Christ will make your hearts strong, blameless, and holy when you stand before God our Father on that day when our Lord Jesus comes with all those who belong to him. (1 Thessalonians 3: 9–13, NLT)

. . .

But you, dear friends, must continue to build your lives on the foundation of your holy faith. And continue to pray as you are directed by the Holy Spirit.

Live in such a way that God's love can bless you as you wait for the eternal life that our Lord Jesus Christ in his mercy is going to give you. Show mercy to those whose faith is wavering. (Jude 1:20–22, NLT)

CHAPTER 25

Prayers of Obedience

⊠

A STORY ABOUT OBEDIENCE

Chiune Sugihara was born at the start of this century—on January 1, 1900. As a young boy in Japan, he had the dream of becoming the Japanese ambassador to Russia. By the 1930s, he was one step away from his dream as the ambassador to Lithuania.

One morning a huge throng of people gathered outside his home. Sugihara learned these people were Jews who had traveled many miles across treacherous terrain from Poland. Now the crowd sought Sugihara's help for Japanese visas which would permit them to flee the German gestapo.

Three times Sugihara wired Tokyo for permission to provide the visas; three times he was rejected. He had to suddenly choose between the fulfillment of his dream and the lives of the crowd. Sugihara chose to disobey orders and for the next twenty-eight days he wrote visas by hand, barely sleeping or eating. Recalled to Berlin, he was still writing visas and shoving them through the train windows into the hands of refugees who ran alongside. Ultimately his work saved six thousand lives.

Besides being a courageous Japanese, Sugihara was a committed Christian. His remaining days of life were spent selling lightbulbs in Japan. When his story was finally told, his son was asked, "How did your father feel about his choice?" The young man replied, "My father's life was fulfilled. When God needed him to do the right thing, he was available to do it."

Today you may not be asked to disobey your government, but you are asked to obey God's desires in the Bible. Through prayer, we can gain strength for obedience.

Let's pray:

◇

Prayer of Obedience to Put God First

Almighty God, you deserve first place in my life. I desire to seek first your kingdom and your righteousness, and then other things will be added to me. As a man, God, at times my heart is far from putting you first and I seek your help today. I need your aid to establish the proper priorities so that I can do those things which are pleasing to you.

Please, God, I pray that you would help me to never be guilty of idolatry and worshiping human idols. I ask for you to help me to always respond promptly by putting you first in my life. I acknowledge you as the Lord of my life and I also acknowledge that it is in you that I live and move and breathe. I will exalt your name in all the earth, so that other people may see that you are the only thing in life that really matters.

Amen.

◇

Prayer of Obedience in Giving

God, I want to talk with you about an important subject today—my giving. Help me to be obedient to you with my giving of my finances, my talent, and my time. I understand that everything which I have comes from you. I pray that you will help me to remember to give you the first fruits of my labor and my day. You've told me in the Bible how you want me to give the first fruits of my labor to you. Today I purpose in my heart to give tithes and offerings to you on a regular basis.

Lord, I repent of all selfishness that has stopped me from being obedient in this arena of giving. I know that you will supply all of my needs according to your riches in glory by Christ Jesus. Direct me in my giving to the place that you desire. Bless my giving, I pray, O God, so that I may be glorified by my obedience to your will.

Amen.

◇

Prayer for Obedience to Pray

Dear God, help me to become obedient in prayer. I do not want to lose this desire to talk with you on a regular basis. At times, Heavenly Father, I am tempted to grow weary in prayer. It seems that at times, my patience is exhausted and I become discouraged in prayer. Help me, Dear Lord, to persevere in prayer and to come with greater confidence and boldness before you.

I thank you, God, that your word tells me that I can have confidence in you, if I pray anything according to your will, you hear me: and if you hear me, I can be assured that, whatsoever I ask, I know that I have the answers that I desired of you. Sometimes that answer to my prayer comes immediately and other times the answer is unexpected and still other times the answer is wait. Give me the grace to continue in prayer and wait patiently for your answer.

Help me, Lord, to fully understand that the earnest, heart-felt and continued prayer of a righteous man makes tremendous power available. Help me to understand that when I am obedient to prayer, you, Father, are honored and glorified. Thank you for teaching me on a continual basis about prayer and how to grow in my obedience to the discipline of prayer.

Amen.

⊠

Prayer for Obedience

Dear God, I confess that at times I am very disobedient to you. I know that you know what is best for me. Sometimes it's not easy for me to obey your word and to have faith in your direction for my life.

I thank you, God, that your word declares that if I am faithful to confess my sins to you that you will be faithful to forgive my sins. Help me, God, to live a life that is pleasing to you. Help me to be obedient to you in every way and in every situation, so that my life might bring glory to your name. I pray that I will walk in your ways and keep your statutes and obey you rather than man.

Dear Lord, it is important to me that others see your life in me. Let it be, O God, that I will honor you as a man who lives in obedience with your Word.

Amen.

◇

BIBLE VERSES ABOUT OBEDIENCE

Carefully obey every command I give you today. Then you will live and grow in number, and you will enter and take the land the Lord promised your ancestors.

Remember how the Lord your God has led you in the desert for these forty years, taking away your pride and testing you, because he wanted to know what was in your heart. He wanted to know if you would obey his commands. He took away your pride when he let you get hungry, and then he fed you with manna, which neither you nor your ancestors had ever seen. This was to teach you that a person does not live by eating only bread, but by everything the Lord says.

During these forty years, your clothes did not wear out, and your feet did not swell. Know in your heart that the Lord your God corrects you as a parent corrects a child.

Obey the commands of the Lord your God, living as he has commanded you and respecting him. (Deuteronomy 8:1–6, NCV)

Then if my people, who are called by my name, are sorry for what they have done, *if they pray and obey me and stop their evil ways, I will hear them from heaven.* I will forgive their sin, and I will heal their land. Now I will see them, and I will listen to the prayers prayed in this place. (2 Chronicles 7:14–15, NCV)

For this reason, *all who obey you should pray to you* while they still can. When troubles rise like a flood, they will not reach them. You are my hiding place. You protect me from my troubles and fill me with songs of salvation. Selah.

The Lord says, "I will make you wise and show you where

to go. I will guide you and watch over you. So don't be like a horse or donkey, that doesn't understand. They must be led with bits and reins, or they will not come near you."

Wicked people have many troubles, but the Lord's love surrounds those who trust him. Good people, rejoice and be happy in the Lord. Sing all you whose hearts are right. (Psalm 32:6–11, NCV)

So the supervisors and governors went as a group to the king and said: "King Darius, live forever! The supervisors, assistant governors, governors, the people who advise you, and the captains of the soldiers have all agreed that you should make a new law for everyone to obey: For the next thirty days no one should pray to any god or human except to you, O king. *Anyone who doesn't obey will be thrown into the lions' den.*

"Now, O king, make the law and sign your name to it so that it cannot be changed, because then it will be a law of the Medes and Persians and cannot be canceled." So King Darius signed the law.

Even though Daniel knew that the new law had been written, he went to pray in an upstairs room in his house, which had windows that opened toward Jerusalem. Three times each day Daniel would kneel down to pray and thank God, just as he always had done.

Then those men went as a group and found Daniel praying and asking God for help. So they went to the king and talked to him about the law he had made. They said, "Didn't you sign a law that says no one may pray to any god or human except you, O king? Doesn't it say that anyone who disobeys during the next thirty days will be thrown into the lions' den?"

The king answered, "Yes, that is the law, and the laws of the Medes and Persians cannot be canceled."

Then they said to the king, "Daniel, one of the captives from Judah, is not paying attention to you, O king, or to the law you signed. Daniel still prays to his God three times every day." The king became very upset when he heard this. He wanted to save Daniel, and he worked hard until sunset trying to think of a way to save him.

Then those men went as a group to the king. They said, "Remember, O king, the law of the Medes and Persians says that no law or command given by the king can be changed." So King Darius gave the order, and Daniel was brought in and thrown into the lions' den. The king said to Daniel, "May the God you serve all the time save you!" (Daniel 6:6–16, NCV)

My dear friends, *you have always obeyed God when I was with you. It is even more important that you obey now while I am away from you.* Keep on working to complete your salvation with fear and trembling, because God is working in you to help you want to do and be able to do what pleases him.

Do everything without complaining or arguing. Then you will be innocent and without any wrong. You will be God's children without fault. But you are living with crooked and mean people all around you, among whom you shine like stars in the dark world. (Philippians 2:12–15, NCV)

CHAPTER 26

Prayers for Others: Intercessory Prayers

⊠

A Story About Intercessory Prayer

Lee Grady's wife, Deborah, says that occasionally he snores at night—but she's never proven it to him with a tape recorder. Also Deborah says the editorial director at *Charisma* occasionally laughs in his sleep—another biblical quality, because Psalm 149: 5 (NASB) says, "The righteous will sing for joy on their beds." It wasn't until recently that Lee actually prayed in his sleep.

One night about three A.M., Lee woke up with a deep sense of God's presence. Suddenly Lee felt that he had been praying for his pastor, Carl, and his two college-age sons, Peter and Andrew. In his mind, he replayed in Technicolor a scene where these two young men were, on their knees at the church altar. Other people were gathered around them, laying their hands on them and praying. In the darkness of his bedroom, Lee realized that God was doing something profound in his pastor's family.

Then Lee was struck with the fact that the prayers didn't originate with him. He had no information about the spiritual needs of Peter and Andrew, but the Holy Spirit was interceding for them. For some reason, Lee was recruited to agree with God's will for these two young men. He knew that the Holy Spirit was praying through him. It reminded him of the words of the Apostle Paul when he wrote about the supernatural work of prayer: "For we do not know how to pray as we should, but the Spirit Himself intercedes for us with groanings too deep for words." (Romans 8:26b, NASB)

As I encourage you to pray for others, I'm not advocating a new fad of "sleep-praying." Instead, as men, we need to understand the Lord's desire for us to pray and bring about God's perfect plan for another person. As we pray for others, we begin a special work called "intercession." This special ministry can transpire anytime and anyplace. It doesn't take any special equipment—just a heart yielded to God and open to considering the needs of others before our own. Admittedly it's a strange attitude in this self-centered world where we claw our way to the top of the corporate ladder. Yet the process of intercession helps us get a closer connection to our Heavenly Father.

Let's pray:

⊗

Prayer of Intercession for Your Local Church Leader

Bless the leaders of our church, Dear God, that they might serve you according to your divine will. Fill our pastor(s), elders, and other church leaders with the knowledge of your will and direction.

Lord, I pray that they will be strengthened with might by the power of your Holy Spirit. Pour out your abundant grace upon them that they may speak the truth in love so that they may grow in you through all things. Grant that their families are blessed with unconditional love and harmony. Prosper them in all their ways and bless them financially. Release your ordained helpers into their lives so they will not be overcome, overwhelmed, or wear in well-doing.

Thank you, Lord, for your hand of grace in their lives. Give them boldness and courage and uphold them with your righteous right hand. I pray that as my pastor(s) wait on you, Lord, that you will strengthen their heart, for their hope is in you.

Amen.

⬦

Prayer for the Nation

God, in your Word you say, if your people, who are called by your name, are sorry for what they have done, if they pray and obey you and stop their evil ways, they will hear from heaven. And you will forgive their sin and heal their land. God, I pray a special prayer today for my nation, that you would bring healing to our land and to its people. Heavenly Father, we know that our fight is not against people on the earth but against the rulers and authorities and powers of this world's darkness, against the spiritual powers of evil in the heavenly realm.

Grant your mercy to be poured out on this nation so that you might be glorified throughout the land. God, I know that you will always give what is right to your people who cry to you night and day. Thank you that you promise that you are not slow to answer them. Bless this nation and all that call on your name.

Amen.

⊗

Prayer for the National Political Leadership

Father God, I pray for ——— that he/she would be a just leader who rules in the fear of God. Help him/her to be a leader of wisdom, free from covetousness and immorality, who does not misuse power, position, or possessions. God, I pray that ——— would have a teachable spirit with a heart for the poor and the compassionate. Bless him/her to lead in mercy and in truth, free from bribery and corruption.

Dear Lord, I know that it is your desire that all men be saved and come to the knowledge of the truth. I pray God that ——— will accept your will from his/her life and thereby glorify you. Lord God, as I pray for all who are in authority, I thank you that your promise to me is that I may lead a quiet and peaceable life in all godliness. Thank you that you hear my prayer and thank you for working in the life of this nation's leadership.

Amen.

⊗

Prayer for Other Men

Dear God, I come boldly and with confidence before you. In prayer, I want to stand in the gap for the men of this nation. Lord God, I pray that men would hear your voice and surrender to your call to become watchmen on the walls of this nation. I pray that they would never be silent, day or night, but would call on your name until you establish this nation and make them the praise of the earth.

I ask you, Lord, to grant these men courage to never be ashamed of the Gospel of Jesus Christ. With confidence, these men will lift their voice and not be afraid. You are the awesome, the great King over all the earth. Reveal yourself, I pray, to men so that your name may be exalted in the earth. For the earth is yours and everything in it. Rise up, O God, for the men are your inheritance. Amen.

⌧

BIBLE VERSES ABOUT INTERCESSION

So Daniel went to King Nebuchadnezzar and asked for an appointment so that he could tell the king what his dream meant. Then Daniel went to his house and explained the whole story to his friends Hananiah, Mishael, and Azariah. *Daniel asked his friends to pray* that the God of heaven would show them mercy and help them understand this secret so he and his friends would not be killed with the other wise men of Babylon.

During the night God explained the secret to Daniel in a vision. Then Daniel praised the God of heaven. Daniel said: "Praise God forever and ever, because he has wisdom and power. He changes the times and seasons of the year. He takes away the power of kings and gives their power to new kings. He gives wisdom to those who are wise and knowledge to those who understand. He makes known secrets that are deep and hidden; he knows what is hidden in darkness, and light is all around him.

"I thank you and praise you, God of my ancestors, because you have given me wisdom and power. You told me what we asked of you; you told us about the king's dream." (Daniel 2:16–23, NCV)

˒

Prophecy about Jesus Christ:

But it was the Lord's good plan to crush him and fill him with grief. Yet when his life is made an offering for sin, he will have a multitude of children, many heirs. He will enjoy a long life, and the Lord's plan will prosper in his hands. When he sees all that is accomplished by his anguish, he will be satisfied. And because of what he has experienced, my righteous servant will make it possible for many to be counted righteous, for he will bear all their sins.

I will give him the honors of one who is mighty and great, because he exposed himself to death. He was counted among those who were sinners. *He bore the sins of many and interceded for sinners.* (Isaiah 53:10–12, NLT)

Anyone who is having troubles should pray. Anyone who is happy should sing praises. Anyone who is sick should call the church's elders. They should pray for and pour oil on the person in the name of the Lord. And the prayer that is said with faith will make the sick person well; the Lord will heal that person. And if the person has sinned, the sins will be forgiven.

Confess your sins to each other and *pray for each other* so God can heal you. When a believing person prays, great things happen. Elijah was a human being just like us. He prayed that it would not rain, and it did not rain on the land for three and a half years! Then Elijah prayed again, and the rain came down from the sky, and the land produced crops again. (James 5:13–18, NCV)

CHAPTER 27

Prayers in Secret

⊠

A STORY ABOUT PRAYERS IN SECRET

Deep in the Arabian desert lies a small fortress which stands silently on the vast expanse of sand. Thomas Edward Lawrence, known as Lawrence of Arabia, often came to this fortress. Though unpretentious, it was sufficient and its primary feature was the security.

Whenever under attack, often from superior forces, Lawrence would retreat there. He took over the resources of the fortress. The food and water which he had stored were life-supporting and the strength of the fortification became the strength of its occupants.

Old desert-dwellers around the fortress recall that Sir Lawrence felt confident and secure inside the walls. He learned to trust the secret fortress and his experience proved its worth. Like that fort, "The Lord is good, a stronghold in the day of trouble; and He knows them that trust in him." Through prayer, we can enter God's secret fortress.

Psalm 91 reminds us, "He that dwells in the secret place of the Most High shall dwell in safety." Prayer can occur in a public setting such as a house of worship or another place with other people. Our prayers in secret retain a special quality because they are private and involve spending time alone with our Heavenly Father. We don't get any recognition or pats on the back for our prayers in secret. Instead, we turn to God for our communication, and in secret, the Lord reinforces our lives with his presence.

Let's pray:

⬦

Prayer for Freedom from Fear

Father, I thank you that you are the light of my salvation and that your perfect love casts out fear. God, you know that at times, I struggle as a man with the fear of inadequacy. This fear is robbing me of faith. Please release me, I pray, by your powerful might and I shall be free. It is not your will that I live in fear, because it is your pleasure to give me peace.

Lord, you are my refuge and my strength. Even though I walk through the valley of the shadow of death, I will fear no evil for you are always with me. Your rod and your staff, they comfort me.

Amen.

⬦

Prayer to Live in Humility

God, I want to admit that I'm often full of pride and arrogance. In this world where you have to fight to the top, it's a pattern that I often fall into—and I am without excuse. Father, help me to not be wise in my own eyes but to submit to your guidance in my life. I want to live humbly as your servant.

Your Word admonishes me that I should do nothing through vain glory, but in lowliness of mind hold up others better than myself. Help me to be a man of humility so that my prayers will be answered and you will be lifted up in my life.

Amen.

⊗

Prayer to Conquer My Thoughts

Heavenly Father, I come into your presence and ask that you would help me with my thought life. I want my thoughts to be in accordance with your thoughts and your Word. You know the thoughts that I think in secret because as the Almighty God nothing is hidden about me from you. You know my inner thoughts and secret actions.

Search me, O God, and know my heart and my thoughts, and see if there is anything wicked in me. If so, I ask for you to remove such evil in my life and help me to follow you with my whole heart.

Thank you for your great love for me and for assisting me as I submit my thought-life to you.

Amen.

⊗

Prayer for Loneliness

God, I am a lonely man. Teach me, I pray, when I feel alone. Father God, I pray that you would remove this spirit of loneliness from me. Help me to remember that you are always with me and will never leave or forsake me.

Grant me to hold fast to the profession of my faith and realize that you are touched with the feelings of my infirmities. May I continue to believe and trust in your ability to provide for my every need. In you, Dear God, I will seek comfort.

Amen.

⬦

Prayer to Overcome Lust

Dear God, I am aware that lust leads to sin yet I am a man who is captive to lusts. Lusts have created many problems in my life. Help me, I pray, to resist temptations by making a way of escape for me, so that I will be able to bear it.

Empower me, Almighty God, to flee from lust and the very appearance of evil. Help me to be a man who follows after righteousness, faith, and love. Grant me the ability not to love the world or the things in the world. Instead help me to love you forever.

Amen.

⬦

BIBLE VERSES ABOUT PRAYERS IN SECRET

"And now about prayer. When you pray, don't be like the hypocrites who love to pray publicly on street corners and in the synagogues where everyone can see them. I assure you, that is all the reward they will ever get.

"But when you pray, go away by yourself, shut the door behind you, and *pray to your Father secretly. Then your Father, who knows all secrets, will reward you.*

"When you pray, don't babble on and on as people of other religions do. They think their prayers are answered only by repeating their words again and again. Don't be like them, because your Father knows exactly what you need even before you ask him!" (Matthew 6:5–8, NLT)

Later, when Jesus was alone, the twelve apostles and others around him asked him about the stories. Jesus said, "*You can know the secret about the kingdom of God.* But to other people I tell everything by using stories so that: 'They will look and look, but they will not learn. They will listen and listen, but they will not understand. If they did learn and understand, they would come back to me and be forgiven.'" (Mark 4:10–12, NCV)

I may speak in different languages of people or even angels. But if I do not have love, I am only a noisy bell or a crashing cymbal. I may have the gift of prophecy. I may understand all *the secret things of God* and have all knowledge, and I may have faith so great I can move mountains. But even with all these things, if I do not have love, then I am nothing. I may give away everything I have, and I may even give my body as an offering to be burned. But I gain nothing if I do not have love. (1 Corinthians 13:1–3, NCV)

Also pray for us that God will give us an opportunity to tell people his message. *Pray that we can preach the secret that God has made known about Christ.* This is why I am in prison. Pray that I can speak in a way that will make it clear, as I should. (Colossians 4:3–4, NCV)

Also pray for me that when I speak, God will give me words so that I can tell the secret of the Good News without fear. I have been sent to preach this Good News, and I am doing that now, here in prison. Pray that when I preach the Good News I will speak without fear, as I should. (Ephesians 6:19–20, NCV)

CHAPTER 28

Some Final Thoughts About Prayer

⊠

As I've learned about prayer in my own life, the journey has been a process with great rewards. Numerous books have highlighted the benefits as you become a man of prayer. For me, the greatest benefit has been the relationship between myself and my Heavenly Father. In prayer, I bring my requests not to the world but to God's ears. In response, God reaches into my life and blesses me in every way.

Across the nation, men are discovering firsthand the benefits of prayer. I've seen many men kneeling at the altar of prayer at Promise Keepers events in stadiums throughout the country. In my own experience, I have found the blessings and triumphs of prayer. During the spring of 1993, my wife and I began to hold a small prayer meeting on Thursday evenings in our home. Friends and family came who wanted to have a deeper relationship with Father God. Now, four years later, I can see how God responded in miraculous ways from our prayer meetings. Through prayer, men received direction for their lives; families were healed and young people developed a hunger for God. Our meetings had one agenda—prayer.

After months of prayer, I sensed that God was directing me to attend an upcoming Promise Keepers event. I learned about Promise Keepers through a radio announcement which described the 1993 Face-to-Face Conference in Boulder, Colorado. It was before Promise Keepers had spread to stadiums across the nation, and had an annual event at Folsom Stadium on the University of Colorado campus.

I had no knowledge of other men in my area who might attend the rally so I prayed and asked God to direct my plans. The radio announcement gave a local church phone number to coordinate my housing with four other men: Bob, Steve (another Steve), Gary, and Thomas. We called ourselves the "double Oreo" because three of us were African-American and two were white brothers. Throughout the Promise Keepers weekend, we spent a considerable amount of time together, getting acquainted and praying.

On the final evening of the conference, Coach Bill McCartney, founder of Promise Keepers, held a single candle. Each of the fifty thousand men received a similar candle when entering the final service. From man to man, the candles were lit throughout the stadium until over fifty thousand men lifted their candles toward heaven. In this ocean of men and lights, I felt overwhelmed from what I sensed to be God's heart for men in prayer. Our Heavenly Father longs for men to become men of prayer and establish a united front for God's will on the earth. It begins with prayer. Ezekiel 22:30 (NLT) says, "I searched for someone who might stand in the gap in the wall so I wouldn't have to destroy the land, but I found no one."

Today God continues to search for men to stand in the gap through prayer. This verse from the prophet presents a clarion call for men to become men of prayer.

After that 1993 Promise Keepers conference, I returned to Houston with a fresh dedication to stir men of our nation about prayer. Our group of five men became the first Houston-area task force for Promise Keepers. Over the next two years, we met each week and prayed together. Little did I know in 1995, God would call me to lead a national prayer initiative for Promise Keepers.

To date, by the grace of God, I have been instrumental in recruiting millions of people to pray for Promise Keepers conferences and other events. It continues to be my passion to stir men beyond their routine life and into a life which is centered in prayer.

In your hands, you hold a new tool to start your journey toward reaching God and becoming a man of prayer. As you use these prayers for your own life, I pray you will expand them and grow in your personal communication with the Creator of the Universe. Together, let's commit ourselves afresh to become men with a commitment to prayer.